From Black and White to Colour

How You Can Be Led By The Holy Spirit

Karen Way

malcolm down
PUBLISHING

First published 2022 by Malcolm Down Publishing Ltd.
www.malcolmdown.co.uk

24 23 22 22   7 6 5 4 3 2 1

British Library Cataloguing in Publication Data
A catalogue record for this book is available from the British Library.

ISBN 978-1-915046-55-0

Names have been changed to protect identities

Contents

Chapter One: New Life

My story begins back in the spring of 1986. Spring is one of my favourite times of year, when the bulbs are pushing up through the soft brown earth, or the lone daffodil has just forced its way through a crack in the path, determined to reach the light. Buds are forming on the trees, getting ready to burst into life, there's beautiful blossom adorning the fruit trees, like lace on a dress, the lambs on my father's farm are being born… such an exciting, expectant time, with new life everywhere.

This spring I too was expecting. I had a tiny life deep inside, hidden in that secret place. I was pregnant with my third child, and I was already the mother of two little girls. I was twenty-five years old, married, and my husband and I had a printing company which we ran together in West Sussex, where we lived.

We had just moved our business into premises which were rented to us by a Christian publishing company that produced a newspaper, the *Christian Herald*,[1] and several Christian magazines.

We ourselves were not Christians, only visiting church for weddings, christenings or funerals. My only experience of church was while I was away at boarding school. We would attend Sunday morning service, walking the short distance to the little stone church just over the road. We would walk in pairs, dressed in our uniform, wearing blazers and hats, and would join the parishioners from the village.

Of course, we were not allowed to talk in church, so when it came to singing hymns my friend and I had made up a way to have a conversation with each other. We would sing the words to each other in the tune of the hymn that was being sung, which always amused us, as sometimes the services seemed very long.

---

1. The publication ceased in 2006.

Aged eleven, I joined the confirmation[2] class that was run midweek in the late afternoon, in order to dodge an extra French lesson. Instead, we would go to the rectory for tea, which was always splendid, with cake and sandwiches, which was much better than the school tea. It was more like the one in the staff room. It really was enjoyed by the small group of girls who attended those classes with me.

After tea, we would sit and listen to the vicar as he went through the many scriptures pertaining to confirmation. We were told that when we were christened as babies our parents had made a promise and we were now confirming that promise, never really sure of what that promise was. We were then given scriptures to go away and read. I was dyslexic but had not been diagnosed. I would open the Bible but I could hardly read the words, and what I did manage to read may as well have been written in a foreign language. I could not understand it.

However, the times at the rectory were always enjoyable. We felt welcome, as the vicar and his wife always seemed pleased to see us. It was sad when those classes ended, but we still had our confirmation service to look forward to, which was going to be held in a much bigger church in town where we would be joined by others who were to be confirmed. We were going to wear white dresses, and we would also be given a present – a cross to wear, or a Bible. We would then be joined by our families and go out to celebrate.

The day of the confirmation service was to be later in the afternoon, so in the hours leading up to it, we were sent outside into the school grounds with a Bible and a paper with a list of scriptures on it, which we were to contemplate. We were not allowed to sit together, so we could not talk, but were sent to different parts of the school grounds.

I was just outside the field where we played hockey, sitting in the long

---

2. Confirmation is a special service that confirms promises made at baptism. It is practised in some Christian denominations, including the Anglican Church.

grass. I remember I saw little daisies growing. I opened my Bible, the thin paper making a rustling sound, and all I could see was pages and pages of black-print, tiny letters. The thought of trying to read them filled me with dread, so instead, seduced by the beautiful little flowers, I decided to pick them and make daisy chains.

I do, however, remember praying to the Lord and apologising for not reading my Bible and thanked him for all the daises. I had my Bible open in case someone came to check up on me.

So, these were my experiences of church and Christianity. And my final touch of Christianity was my wonderful grandfather, Dar as we used to call him. He was a retired vicar and had christened me as a baby. He had come to live with my family in his final years. I don't really ever remember him talking about God other than one conversation with my two older brothers and I, when one of my brothers asked him if there was really a heaven, and in the event of his death, could Dar please send a letter to let us know if heaven did in fact exist? I think my grandfather did leave a letter... he left his big family Bible.

As a child I would talk to God, but a very distant God, or one that lived in the church.

Now, as an adult, and married, our printing company was starting to do a lot of work for our new landlords. It worked well for them as they had got, in effect, an in-house printer, and in return, it gave us a lot of business. They were always very polite, and a pleasant customer to deal with.

The months were passing fast and the tiny life growing inside me was not so tiny any more! I felt huge; there really was not a lot of space left for the baby to grow. The baby had its legs tucked up, and always seemed to have a heel kicked up under my ribs. I remember thinking, not much longer now and I would be able to share this new life with everyone.

Autumn had arrived, another of my favourite seasons. I remember there was a crispness in the air; the trees must have felt the chill and, almost before my very eyes, given a shiver and had started to drop their now beautifully coloured leaves – red, yellow, orange and brown, all bright and vibrant. Each leaf could have told its own story, having lived through the hot summer months. Now the coloured leaves, signalling the end of a season, were lying on the ground making a tapestry carpet, ready to be walked on, rustling beneath our feet.

I too was coming into a new season. I went for my final check-up at the hospital to be told that I had already started to go into labour, and I should ask my husband to bring in my overnight bag, or go home and come straight back. I decided to go home as I wanted to see my little girls and tell them that Mummy was going to hospital, and that I would be back soon with the baby.

My husband then drove us to the hospital, as my contractions got stronger. Some hours later, our son was born. He was gorgeous. He was a very long baby and was obviously going to be very tall. My husband was delighted to have a son, but he did say even if it was another girl he would have been just as delighted. He was so proud that he went up and down the ward, telling everyone, 'It's a boy, it's a boy! we have a son!' whether they wanted to know or not.

A good family friend, Harry, who seemed to be around on all family occasions, arrived and rejoiced with us. Visiting time now over, they left to continue to celebrate the birth of our son well into the night.

I was so tired, but I couldn't sleep. I just lay there and studied my baby's face, his tiny hands and toes, so perfect in every detail. I couldn't wait until next morning when our family would be reunited, and the girls could meet their little brother.

The following morning, I was allowed to go home, and it was arranged that a midwife would visit me later that day. On arriving home, I was greeted by my mother and two very excited little girls. I was then eagerly escorted to the bedroom, where the crib had been decorated with pale-blue ribbon.

I sat on the bed and leant over and placed the baby into the crib. Every five minutes or so, the girls stuffed toys in there, wanting to share with their new brother their well-loved belongings, a soft threadbare rabbit, a teddy bear, sometimes with a bit too much gusto. Stroking him and wanting to hold his little hands, touching him and wanting to kiss him, I think we can say that he was well and truly loved. Then my daughters started climbing all over me. So, it was decided that it was perhaps a good time for my husband to take the girls out for a while, so I could get some much-needed rest.

I closed the door behind them and lay on my bed, looking at my son as he slept. I was unable to keep my eyes open and I soon fell into a deep sleep. It only seemed like a few minutes later that I heard someone knocking at the door.

I jumped up. It was the midwife coming to check on the baby as promised. She said that he looked a little jaundiced and that she would come back later to check on him again.

I showed her to the door and went back into the sitting room. I laid the baby into the Moses basket, which was on the sofa. I was just about to sit down when he made a little sound. I glanced at him, and he looked a little blue. I picked him up and realised it was getting worse. I ran with him to the phone and called an ambulance.

I thought they would tell me what to do. I was so scared to give him mouth-to-mouth in case I did more harm. I was so frightened I couldn't even look at him.

I remember holding him over my shoulder and looking back at him in the mirror on the wall. I could see he was now a navy colour. The ambulancemen arrived within minutes, as in fact the ambulance station was nearby – although it had seemed like hours. When they arrived, the baby had already started breathing again.

My husband and the girls arrived back just as the ambulance was about to leave, so it was agreed that my husband would follow the ambulance to the hospital to be with our son. I was in shock, I was shaking, and would go on later with my mother once we had someone to look after the girls. My husband phoned as soon as he got to the hospital to say that the baby had stopped breathing again in the ambulance.

The thought of being alone with him was terrifying. What if he stopped breathing again and even worse, died? I was even starting to feel afraid of loving him; this was totally irrational. I couldn't risk loving him and then losing him.

Eventually my mother came over, we dropped the girls off with my sister and went to the hospital. I cried and begged my mother: 'Please don't make me take him home, I am so afraid of it happening again.'

What if it happened one night when we were asleep and we lost him? Of course, I was not being rational. I was just talking out of fear of the thought of it all happening again and losing him; it was more than I could bear.

After arriving at the hospital, still shaking, I was met by my husband who took hold of my hand and reassured me that the doctors were doing their best to find out what was wrong with our little boy. He then turned to me and said, 'Our son needs us to be strong!' but I was not feeling strong, I was just so afraid.

We then went into the room filled with doctors and nurses all around him; he was in an incubator, his little head had been shaved and there were tubes everywhere, and a drip. I could hear the sound of a monitor; there was an urgency in the air as doctors were giving out lists of tests that needed to be run.

My husband, still holding my hand, told me that I needed to touch our son and let him know that I was there. I placed my hand into the incubator, where he lay just dressed in a nappy, and I stroked his soft little body. When I spoke to him, telling him that Mummy and Daddy were there now, he smiled. I know they say that babies don't smile at that age, but he did.

Later we were given a room nearby, with a camp bed so we could stay with him, as we still didn't know what was wrong or what the outcome would be. Although we were both exhausted, we were aware that we needed to call my husband's parents, who had recently moved to Lincolnshire, to tell them what was going on. I will always remember what my mother-in-law said to me: 'I will pray.' She was not a religious woman, but her mother had been, and she must have heard her say it at times of crisis. Those words suddenly became alive to me: 'I will pray.'

Suddenly I was thinking of God, his goodness, and healing I had heard of through our Christian landlords.

I knew I needed to pray to God, to ask him to heal our baby and to save his life. So that is what I did. I prayed and asked God to please make him well. If he did, I would even go to church; in some naïve way I thought that would help.

Within a few days, our baby was improving as the cocktail of antibiotics were beginning to work. I was still afraid to be on my own with him in case he stopped breathing again. The doctor kept saying he was 'a missed cot death'. I didn't want to take him home without some sort of alarm in case he stopped breathing while we were asleep.

About a week after he was admitted, one of the nurses told us they had the test results back. Apparently, they had grown some cultures from swabs taken from the umbilical cord. When the cord had been cut, an infection had set in and because he was so immature, his immune system had not been able to fight it. My husband remembered that after our son's birth the scissors were dropped and then picked up to cut the cord. My poor baby, but at least we now knew the reason for him being so ill. No wonder the doctor didn't think we needed an alarm to go home with, he was not a 'missed cot death'; he was a baby that had nearly died because of a mistake made during his birth.

I knew that God had saved him and I always meant to go to church to thank him. Church, in my mind, was where God lived. But I never seemed to find the time to go to church; life was now so busy with three small children under four.

Months passed and I decided to find someone to look after the children at home a few days a week so I could then go into the print workshop. I could help with answering the phone, delivering print and seeing clients about different jobs. We were getting a lot more Christian customers and one was to change the course of my life forever.

One of the days that I was helping I had arrived an hour later than my husband, which was not unusual as I would have to sort out the children before coming into work.

On arriving, my husband was busy. The printing machine was running, the air was filled with a lovely aroma of fresh coffee percolating in the corner, mixed with the smell of printing ink, and the paper delivery had just arrived, so there were huge reams of paper piled up high. The phone was already ringing, so I just ran to the office to answer it. It was one of our newest customers, Challenge Literature.[3] They were phoning to enquire when their job would be finished, so I asked them to hold the line while I went to see. In fact, it was the leaflet that was on the printing machine and I asked my husband when they could have it as they seemed to be in a hurry. He replied that later on that day, once it was printed; it would have to be left for the ink to dry before it was cut.

I relayed the message, and they seemed pleased.

---

3. No longer in business with this name.

After a few more phone calls I poured us a coffee, and with my mug in hand, I perched on a stool near the printing machine.

It was a long run, with hundreds of these little leaflets coming out of the machine. I asked my husband if I could have one to read, interested in what our new customer was having printed. He passed me one of the sheets of paper as there were in fact two on one page.

I began to read the little leaflet. It grabbed my attention straight away it was an amazing short story of how a young mother of three young children had just given birth to her fourth baby and only a few weeks later had been diagnosed with breast cancer – it was really advanced. But through prayer and medical treatment, she was healed, and she was wanting to share her story to encourage others. It was an amazing story, about knowing God's hand on her life and how her faith in a loving God had got her though.

I was myself very encouraged by her story; I could see the love of a compassionate God reach down and touch her not only for wonderful healing, but throughout her difficult journey of treatment.

The little leaflet then went on to tell the reader that if they wanted to know more about this God, there was a little booklet called *Journey into Life* written by Norman Warren.[4] I recognised this was the same loving God that had only a few months before reached down and touched our little son. I really wanted to know more. I asked if my husband if he would please ask for the booklet when he delivered the job. But he said he could not – firstly, because they would think he just wanted it to get more print, and secondly, he said it was too embarrassing. But I could not stop thinking about the story I had just read; I had a desire to know more about this loving God. So, I thought of our landlords… but I knew that it might be too embarrassing to ask them as well. So who could

---

4. First issue 1964. Norman Warren, *Journey into Life*, new edition (Eastbourne: Kingsway Publications 2013)

we ask? Suddenly I remembered our friend who ran an estate agent's business. He was someone that we both knew personally, and I knew went to church. So I invited him to dinner the next night, not wanting to waste any time.

The next evening our friend came to dinner. The children were now all in bed, so we sat down, had our meal and chatted about all sorts of things – the property market, the children and then finally the business, which gave me an opportunity to tell him about the leaflet we had just printed, and how they referred to a little booklet called *Journey into Life*. I asked him if he knew of it. He did. I then asked him if he could perhaps get me one, to which he replied he would. Delighted by his answer, I said I looked forward to receiving it.

The very next morning our friend, who must have had one at home, dropped it off on his way into work, so there it was, sitting on our doormat at 7.30 a.m.

So excited at seeing the booklet, I decided I would try to read it when the children were playing, which later on I did.

I sat in the playroom as the girls, for the first time that day, seemed to play together without fighting over toys, and the baby slept. I opened the little booklet and I started to read. It began with how in the beginning God made humankind, how we fell into sin, and talked about what sin is and how it affects our lives, why Jesus came into the world, forgiveness of sin, and finally leading into a prayer, asking Jesus to come and live in the reader's heart and to walk with us for the rest of our lives.

Over the next few weeks, I read the booklet over and over again. I had told the Lord when our baby was so sick in the hospital that I would go to church. Now I was telling him that I was still meaning to go to church!

Around three weeks later, I remember it was a beautiful sunny day, and our estate agent friend had come for Sunday lunch. We had decided to take a drive out to a little village at the foot of the South Downs in

West Sussex. On arriving, we unloaded the car and went for a walk through the village and then planned to walk beside the river. We were walking through the village, admiring the beautiful little cottages with their well-kept gardens filled with colourful shrubs and plants in the early summer sunshine – it was a wonderful sight; every garden was a picture of beauty and just when you thought it couldn't get any better, it would. As we were coming to the end of the little lane, on the left-hand side up on the hill stood the village church.

I said to my husband, who was pushing the double buggy with our sleeping son, and our friend, who was now walking hand-in-hand with the girls, that I just wanted to go up to the church and that I wouldn't be long. They should continue on towards the river walk, and I would catch them up.

I walked up the path towards the church. On arriving, I opened the big heavy door and went in. It was a little cold, and I could smell the faint aroma of incense in the air. The church was completely empty; it was silent. The only sound was me, as I walked up the aisle towards the front of the church. I reached the step before the altar and knelt down. I began to pray.

The first thing I said was, 'I told you I would come!' – and here I was. I wanted to thank the Lord for healing my little son. I also wanted to thank him for our business premises and our landlords. I then went on to talk to him about the booklet I had read, and said that I was sorry for all the things that I had done wrong in my life, and I asked for his forgiveness. I needed him as my Saviour, and finally, would he please come and live in my heart?

And that is just what he did!

I didn't see the heavens open with a choir of angelic beings singing hallelujah or see fireworks or stars. No, everything in that little church was just the same, but I knew that when I stood up, *I* was not the same.

As I walked out of that church, I knew that I didn't walk out alone.

Now outside, the sun was still shining; I could feel its warmth on my back and head.

As I walked down the path towards the lane, I saw my family in the distance, and then I ran to catch them up. The first thing I said when I reached them was that I had gone into that church to ask Jesus into my heart. Our friend was delighted.

I had started my journey into life!

Chapter Two: Church

The following week our estate agent friend had invited us to come to his church for the morning service. I would feel at home there as an Anglican church had been my only experience of church in the past, and I had always seen my grandfather wear a dog collar, so the vicar would feel very familiar to me. We left the children in the Sunday school over the road, and I remember thinking to myself, was I dressed in the right things? I was in my Doc Marten boots, jeans and a T-shirt but it was too late to worry about that.

I also remember feeling really excited and nervous at the same time.

We sat in the pews towards the back of the church. It was a very formal service, singing hymns from hymnbooks and having to repeat certain responses from a book.

After the service we were introduced to lots of people – we even knew a few from the publishing company, and some of our other Christian customers. Our friend then went on to ask if we would like a babysitter so we could go to the evening service and meet a lot more younger people, which we both said we would like to do.

When our landlords from our business premises heard that I had become a Christian, they were very excited and asked if I would like to come to their prayer meeting in the morning once a week, which I happily agreed to. I used to go to the prayer meetings, and I met a lot of people there. They gave me information on books, hiring videos, and told me about a toddler group with a Bible study, which I then joined, from another church.

The days that I was at the print workshop different people from the publishers would come and see me, armed with Christian magazines and on one occasion, a new Bible. I would often hire two or three Christian videos a week and listen to tapes. I was so hungry for God and

I just couldn't get enough. I was listening to some of the top preachers in the world, real men and women of faith. I think as a dyslexic person, it was an easy way for me to absorb the information.

I had a little book called *Every Day with Jesus*[5] which I would read morning and night. It had scriptures for the day and then a thought that related to what I had just read; so often the scriptures were relevant to my day.

I heard about being baptised in the Holy Spirit – this relates to the time after Jesus had risen from the dead and gone to heaven, and that God the Father sent another, the Holy Spirit, the 'Counsellor' so that the disciples would not be alone (John 16:7). They were empowered in the upper room at Pentecost, as we read in Acts 2, and given a language that didn't have to learn – it was a divine language.

'Wow!' I remember thinking. I wanted to know this Holy Spirit and I wanted to speak this language which didn't need learning. It would be a secret language from God. How wonderful – when you couldn't think of the words to pray in English, you could pray in this language, and it would be the most perfect prayer for that situation! Or when you wanted to tell the Lord how much you loved him, sometimes your own words weren't enough, and you could use this language as a love language to the Lord.[6] While I was thinking about it, I remembered someone who I had met at a prayer meeting, and I thought if anyone would have the gift of tongues that we read about it 1 Corinthians 12, she would.

So, at the next prayer meeting, I met up with her and asked her about the baptism in the Holy Spirit and did she speak in this language? She replied she did. I asked her if she would like to come to dinner in the week and pray for me to receive this gift, and she was really happy and said she would love to.

---

5. Published by CWR.

6. 1 Corinthians 14:2.

The evening came when my friend came to dinner to pray with me, so my husband decided this would be a great opportunity to go out with a friend for a drink while this took place. Jesus seemed to have filled every area of my life; he was all I talked about; I had been swept of my feet. I was in love with him!

My friend arrived and I hadn't even started to cook supper, so while she read a story to the children, who were all now in bed, I placed the rainbow trout in the oven. I hadn't eaten a thing all day, as I was so excited, and my appetite seemed to have gone. My friend asked if I wanted her to pray before our meal or afterwards. I said that I would like her to pray for me first and then we could celebrate what God had done afterwards with our meal.

I was very excited as I knew the Lord would bless me that very evening. I sat in the chair, and she started to pray for me first in English and then in an unknown language. I didn't speak a word, so she continued to pray but nothing seemed to happen. I felt upset, and she said she would go on praying. As she did, I could hear my name being called in another language. The Lord was calling my name over and over again, calling me to come.

I turned to my friend and told her I knew what she was saying, and I could repeat to her what she had just said. She shouted with excitement, 'You can't be taught so just say back to me the words I have said to you!' So, I did, and then I spoke in an unknown language, and as I did, more words came and she said, 'You had it all the time and you just didn't speak it out!' We then sat down and ate our supper and rejoiced together. It was great, God was true to his word. He had promised this gift and he had given it to me.

When my husband came home, I couldn't wait to tell him what had happened.

That night, after going to bed, I was praying my short sentences in my new language. I woke at 3 a.m. to be sure I could still speak in my new language, and I could. I could at 5 a.m. too, and I could still say the words at 6.45 a.m. I then heard a voice saying to me: 'You have been taught.' I suddenly felt worried – how could I have somehow been taught? I turned to the Bible sitting on my bedside table and opened it randomly.

And this is what I read: 'As for you, the anointing you received from him remains in you, and you do not need anyone to teach you. But as his anointing teaches you about all things and as that anointing is real, not counterfeit – just as it has taught you, remain in him' (1 John 2:27).

Wow! The Bible had suddenly come alive. I knew that the Lord was speaking to me through his Word, the Bible, and that the voice of doubt I had heard was not a voice I recognised. I remembered reading that when someone becomes a Christian Jesus is their shepherd and they are his sheep, and Christians know his voice; they won't follow the voice of a stranger.[7] So, I spoke to the voice I did not know and said, 'You are a liar. Get away from here. It is written…' I then quoted the scripture that I had just read. This is always the way to answer the unknown voice. Jesus said this when tempted in the wilderness.[8] You see, Jesus spoke the Word, the Bible, in response to the tempter. From that time on, my life was never the same again. The Lord started to reveal himself to me daily.

The following night, when I went to bed, I had a dream. I started to see my life, or at least, some significant parts from my childhood. I was one of five children, all very close in age. I was in the middle, the third child. I had two older brothers and two younger sisters. There was only thirteen months between my sister and me. One of the first things I saw in this dream, which was a bit like watching a film, was when my sister was born. She was born at home, with bronchial pneumonia. There were no cots in the hospital for her, so she had to be nursed at home. She

---

7. John 10:1-16.

8. Matthew 4:4.

and my mother were shut up in a bedroom for a month or more. I was looked after by my father and his friend. They also had my two brothers and my grandmother, who was living with us as she was dying of cancer, to look after. The separation from my mother was awful. Apparently, I would not eat or even take a bottle.

In this dream I saw myself as a thirteen-month-old baby in a cot, alone, pale and cold, crying for what seemed like hours, with no one hearing or responding to my call. I then felt a pain right up inside my body. I saw a hand with dark fingers. The pain was so real. I remember thinking, 'What's happening? Jesus, where are you? Please come into this room.' In my dream, I saw Jesus come and pick up the small baby from the cot. He held me, the baby, until I felt warm and safe. His arms were strong, and I felt secure and loved; instead of shaking, feeling cold, I was suddenly warm, with rosy cheeks, sleeping on his shoulder as he walked around the room, never putting the baby down.

The next thing I saw, I was about four years old. I was at the end of the long driveway of my family home. I saw a man walking away down the drive. I was really sad, I was crying and wanted him to turn around, but he just kept walking. 'Please come back!' I thought. 'Don't go.' But he didn't turn back. The next thing that happened was that this man was then bound up with big ropes that were wrapped around him. He couldn't speak and he was then placed in a large cannon. I had no idea what I was seeing or what I had witnessed. I said to the Lord, 'Who is this man? I don't remember him.' And then the name Mr Baker came to mind. Mr Baker sounded familiar, but I could not think who he was, or why he should be walking away.

The final picture I saw, I was eleven years old. The picture was in black and white. It was the day of my confirmation, and I was sitting in the field making daisy chains with my Bible open! But then the picture was no longer black and white, it was in colour, but everything seemed to be brighter, the grass, the daisies. Then I noticed my Bible open on the ground. I could see the tiny black letters. But the same letters that had filled me with dread at the thought of trying to read them had suddenly turned multicoloured.

I was thinking about what I had just seen. It was as if the Bible that I had opened all those years ago had had life breathed into the pages; it was now alive. Just as I had finished looking at this picture in my dream, I awoke – my bedroom door had been flung open. It was the girls, they had come in for their morning cuddles.

'Never mind,' I thought. I decided to ask my mother who the man in my dream might be, as I would be spending the day with her on my parents' farm with the children.

Later in the morning I drove the forty minutes to my mother's home. I prayed in my new language all the way, while the children listened to their music. During the course of a very busy day, while the children were playing, my mother and I were able to sit down with a cup of tea, and talk. I could finally ask my mother the question I had been longing to ask her all day, if she knew the man in my dream? I then described him to her, or at least the back of him: he was short and stout, brown hair and wearing a suit. Who was he? And did she know him?

'Yes,' she said, instantly recognising the man I had described. 'That was Mr Baker.'

'Well, who was he and what happened to him?' I asked.

My mother went on to tell me that he was one of my father's employees. He was one of three reps for my father's wholesale china and glass company. He would come every day to our house, to my father's office. He would bring sweets and play and chat with my siblings and I before going out to work.

'So, what happened to him?' I enquired.

'Well, quiet simply,' said my mother, 'your father fired him.'

'*Fired him!*' I laughed. Of course, you can fire a cannon. And he was bound up with ropes because he had no choice. As a little girl, all I saw was the back of him as he walked down our drive and away.

The Lord showed me that's why I had actually found it hard to believe the gift of the Holy Spirit when I had been given a new language, and the reason why I had kept checking to see that I could still speak in my new language, worried that the Holy Spirit might have left – so many people in my life had come and gone. We had had lots of different nannies while growing up. They would come and then leave or be fired; it was just a natural occurrence.

The Holy Spirit had shown me, however, that he would never leave me. Within a few days of being prayed for, the Holy Spirit had also shown me that he was my teacher, the Bible had become alive, and he was showing me parts of my past life. He had opened my eyes to a whole new realm of my childhood and was healing me. This was just the beginning of my journey with my loving God.

A few days later I went into an empty church, in the morning around 10 a.m. on my way into work; this was the Anglican church that we now attended on a Sunday. I wanted to thank God for all he was doing. I knelt in the silence and started to thank the Lord for his precious Holy Spirit, who was always with me and who was revealing so much to me, not only about my own life, but also introducing me to Jesus and the Father himself and making them so real to me. After I had finished thanking the Lord, I got up and started to walk up the aisle to the door, when suddenly a woman appeared from nowhere. She made me jump as I had thought I was alone. She said that she often came to the church at this time of the day because it was quiet, and she could pray without distractions. I told her I had just become a Christian and that I had just been baptised in the Holy Spirit. She told me that she too had been baptised in the Holy Spirit. God had given her this gift. She then said that she was going to a little Bible study at a friend's house just across the road from the church, and asked if I would like to come with her.

The children were with the childminder, so I called my husband and told him about the Bible study, which would not be much more than an hour. He thought that I should go, and come on to the workshop afterwards, so I agreed to join her.

We walked over the road to a bungalow, up the path and she rang the bell. The door was answered by a lovely old lady called Isabel. She seemed very pleased to see us and made me feel at home in her little sitting room with two pale green sofas, and different wooden chairs she had laid out in preparation for her Bible study. On seeing that she had another person to join in, she went to the kitchen to get another chair.

Others began to arrive; there were about eight of us in all. They all seemed old to me, but it really didn't matter. Isabel led the Bible study, and they each took it in turns to read passages from the Bible and then discuss the text. I didn't have a Bible with me, but I was relieved because I did not like reading out loud. After we had finished the Bible study, we had a cup of coffee and a biscuit from the plate as it was offered around.

Isabel asked if I had enjoyed the Bible study and enquired if I would like to come again, to which I replied, 'I would very much like to come again!' I continued to visit Isabel and we were to become good friends. I would phone her and ask her the meaning of different things I had seen or heard with regards to Jesus. She was amazing, her wonderful knowledge of the Bible and her loving relationship with Jesus, her Saviour, and the many years of wisdom she had gained through walking with God were always a great source of encouragement to me.

It was almost a year from when we had first started to attend the services at the Anglican church that we were to have a pastor from the local Baptist church come to the morning service; he was going to preach. I was very encouraged by his message and his church was just down the road from where we lived, so my husband and I agreed that it would be good idea to visit his church for a Sunday service, as it would be a more charismatic – that is, practising the gifts of the Holy Spirit that we read about in the book of 1 Corinthians. We had really enjoyed the Baptist church service; it was very different to the church we had become used to. We were not singing out of hymn books but the words to the songs were up on a screen in the front of the church; there was also a band and some singers leading the worship. People were lifting their hands as they poured out their worship to God. It was a really different. They were worshipping God and pouring out the same love and adoration to him that I had seen in the Anglican church, only in a more *charismatic* way. I saw that neither way is a better way, as I realised it is your heart that you worship from.

I knew the Anglican church was the right place for me to begin my journey, as it was familiar to me. But now we were moving into a new season in God, and we decided to start attending the Baptist church and make it our new spiritual home. I think the vicar and his wife were sad to see us leave, but understood that it was nearer to where we lived, and with their blessing we left, promising to still visit. I also carried on visiting Isabel and, of course, we still saw many of our friends.

Just a few weeks after joining the church, I remember going on my own to a service called 'Reflections around the cross'. When I arrived, the service had already started, so I crept in and sat at the back. A man was playing the cello and wonderful music and singing filled the air. I remember looking at the people there as they sang, they looked so spiritual. Some had pained expressions on their faces, and I remember, as I looked at them, I said, 'Lord, I am a good actress; I could pull the same expressions and look the same.' But I thought, 'What does the cross mean to me?' As I sat there and closed my eyes, I suddenly saw myself as I was dressed that day, black cords, black T-shirt and my well-loved Doc Marten boots. I was kneeling at the foot of the cross and the blood of Jesus was just washing over me. I remember noticing I was alone, which was strange for me, because I was always part of a crowd, coming from a big family.

The Lord said to me, 'I died for you personally.' The next thing that happened was, as I stood to my feet in my vision, I noticed I was no longer dressed in my black clothes but in a white robe. It was whiter than white, and light like I had never seen before was shining from it all around me.

I didn't see God, but I knew I was in his presence, and I had my hands held out, rather like a waiter. They were held out for service. I knew at that point God had called me.

I left the church and drove the short distance home.

When I arrived home, the first thing I did was to phone Isabel and tell her what had happened in the Baptist church and what I had seen. She went on to tell me what I had seen was in the Bible, and to read Revelation 7:13-15 Then she explained how we, as Christians, are clothed in robes of righteousness, having been washed in the blood of Jesus. God had shown me how to come into his presence through being cleansed by the blood of Christ, and I could come in wearing a robe of righteousness because of what Jesus did for me, on the cross.

I knew that I could have imitated what I had seen in the church, and looked like everyone else, but I needed to be real. I wanted it to be real for me. I had learned if we ask the Holy Spirit, he would show us things and take us right into the presence of God. We then enter a different realm; the Bible and this loving God were real. It was the Holy Spirit who was making it all so real.

Isabel always loved to hear what God was doing in my life, as I too was interested to hear what the Lord was doing in her life. She would also share her favourite scriptures with me, and why they were her favourite; what they meant to her. So now I couldn't wait to read the scriptures she had given me. I opened my Bible and read Revelation 7:13-15:

Then one of the elders asked me, 'These in white robes – who are they, and where did they come from?' I answered, 'Sir, you know.' And he said, 'These are they who have come out of great tribulation; they have washed their robes and made them white in the blood of the Lamb. Therefore, "they are before the throne of God and serve him day and night in his temple; and he who sits on the throne will spread his tent over them."'

That was it! Just what I had seen, it was in the Bible, my Bible was being revealed to me, so far away from that little girl all those years before, sitting in the long grass and daisies with a Bible of tiny black letters – it was now vibrant and full of colour and life. I remember just being filled with such a sense of gratitude and an overwhelming love for the Lord and all he was doing.

We were settling into the Baptist church, making new friends; there were also some of our Christian customers there. I also started to go to some of their prayer meetings. The girls were now both starting school and nursery, so it was new beginnings for all of us.

We had not long been at the Baptist church when one Sunday morning, the pastor was preaching a sermon on being disciples of Jesus. And in closing his message he asked if anyone there wanted to be a disciple of Jesus. My husband had been sitting on the side lines long enough, in his words and now one year on from my own conversion, he said that he too wanted to be a disciple. My husband asked Jesus into his heart. He wanted what he had seen in our Christian friends, and my life. It was a new beginning for him too.

The printing business was growing, so we took on a bookkeeper a few days a week. We also took on another printer part-time. I stayed at home with the children, going into the print workshop less often, and the office only occasionally.

We also joined a house group at our neighbour's home. At the house group we would have a Bible study, where we would take it in turns to read a passage from the Bible. When it came for me to read, I found that fear would grip my heart, I was so afraid. What if I couldn't pronounce the words properly, or even worse, couldn't read the words? I told my husband that I didn't really enjoy going, because of the reading. He was not sure how to help me, so I decided to tell the Lord about it, even though I knew he knew already.

I told the Lord how I felt, and I asked him to please heal me. I didn't care that I couldn't read any book properly, but I needed to know that I could read my Bible.

My mother had told me in the past that I may be dyslexic as I had problems spelling and had taken a long time in learning to read. I can even remember the very first book that I was learning to read as a five-year-old. I remember being so upset that I couldn't read it as everybody else seemed able; even the content of the story had distressed me. I knew that I was different to my peers; what they found so easy was always so hard for me. I suppose I felt I was stupid.

The very next day, I thought my prayer had been answered. A friend of mine told me about a healing meeting that would be taking place at the evening service in an Anglican church in a few days' time. I was really looking forward to it. In the time leading up to the service, I listened to tapes and watched Christian videos; my faith levels were really high. I was expecting a miracle.

The evening of the service came. I was going alone – my husband was going to stay at home with the children. I arrived at the church and decided to sit at the back. The service started with hymns, then the vicar went up into the pulpit and began to speak about healing. The first thing he said was: 'Don't worry if you don't get healed; it might not happen straight away.' He went on to explain how healing comes in different ways. I felt my expectancy for a miracle sink as he spoke about why it might not happen. My faith was totally depleted.

I went through the motions of going up for prayer. A deacon prayed. I felt nothing had happened. After leaving the service, I sat in my car and cried, so disappointed. I just drove around for an hour before I could go home and face my husband. I cried out to God again and asked him to heal me as I felt nothing had happened in the church. A conversation with a church leader about how I should be feeding myself on milk in the Word, as a baby Christian, made me think about the videos and tapes I'd been watching and listening to. Should I perhaps give them up? So that night when I went to bed, I prayed again. Even though it was much easier to get understanding from videos and tapes than trying to read my Bible alone, I did love my Bible. 'Please, will you heal me so I can read my Bible?' I asked. I felt the Lord said he would heal me if I read my Bible from cover to cover! Excited by what I felt the Lord had said, I said I would read my Bible from cover to cover, and then I would go back to my videos and tapes! So that night I began to read my Bible. I was enjoying it, mostly reading at night after children were in bed.

One night my husband and I were in bed. He was reading a book, and I was reading my Bible; having now read Genesis and Exodus, I was more confident. It was becoming easier and easier to read and understand. Then that night I started to read Leviticus, and my heart sank!

I said to the Lord, 'I don't understand it. I can't do this. It's going over the top of my head.'

I heard a voice. I jumped up and went into the girls' bedroom to investigate, only to find them both sound asleep, so I went into our son's room. I peered into his cot, and to my surprise he was awake. I picked him up and carried him to our bedroom, and placed him in between my husband and I; he seemed quite content just to lay there. So, I continued my conversation with the Lord, where I had been telling him it was really hard, and I didn't think I could read my Bible, and how it wasn't going in any more… I couldn't understand it.

Just as I had finished expressing my feelings, my little son spoke! My husband and I, both shocked, turned to each other and then to him. He said, 'Read it, Mummy.' We dropped our books and stared at him. He said it again: 'Read it, Mummy.' We were both astounded as he could only say Dadda before that! My husband asked, 'Why is he saying that? And more than that, he can't talk!'

I believe the Holy Spirit was speaking through him, encouraging me to carry on reading my Bible, which I did over the next weeks and months. God showed me many things and taught me. He healed me! I could now read my Bible in front of anyone. This was another side to my wonderful God… he could speak through a little child. Read about that for yourself in Psalm 8:2! Maybe that vicar was right in that healing service at the Anglican church; it doesn't always happen straight away, and healing comes in many different ways!

This Bible was now so different from the one on my confirmation day; it was filled with life and colour. I was seeing so many things in the Bible happening in my own life. Just when I thought God couldn't show himself to me in a different way, he would.

Now that my husband was a Christian, we were going to a lot more meetings. He had joined the Full Gospel Business Men's Fellowship[9] meetings, which were weekly, and once a month they would invite their wives to a dinner at a hotel. They would have a guest speaker and they were always wonderful evenings, with powerful testimonies.

One of those evening that I remember, we took a friend with us. Like

9. See www.fgbuk.org/ (accessed 27 October 2022).

all the other meetings we had been to, it was a powerful story and then they would have a time of ministry. Well, that night, the speaker had asked people that suffered backaches to come forward and he would pray for them. Our friend told us that she suffered bad back pain, so she went forward, and the speaker asked her to sit on the chair with her feet out in front of her. 'Why?' we wondered. He then said one of her legs was slightly shorter than the other, as he held the two together. He was right, and that was what was throwing her back out of alignment and causing the pain! He then said he would pray for her legs to be the same length. As he prayed, before our eyes, we watched her leg line up with the other one; it had literally grown. We were utterly amazed. After the meeting, we walked to our car and my husband opened the door for her. As she was getting in, she bumped her head, not badly, but she stood back about to re-enter the car when I said, 'You must have misjudged it because you are taller!' And with that we laughed so hard that we couldn't get into the car until we had composed ourselves. I am sure that the Lord was laughing with us too – he has a sense of humour.

We would also go to Brighton, not many miles along the coast from where we lived. A pastor from a local church held outreach meetings, and they were always very exciting; we saw lots of healings. He was also a really good Bible teacher. Mostly he would teach on faith and living in the Spirit; he encouraged me so much. I was so hungry for God that I soaked it up like a dry sponge.

We had a lot of really good babysitters by now, so we could go to all these different meetings. And having so many Christian friends in the publishing company from lots of different churches, we were always being told about different meetings that were going on.

After completing a new members' course at the Baptist church, we both decided that we wanted to be baptised, although we had been christened as babies. We now wanted to make that declaration that as adults we were Christians, and that as we would go down into the water, our sins were washed away, symbolising what had happened by the blood of the Jesus, the Lamb, and we were coming up into new life. This was just to be an outward sign of what had already taken place in our lives. Then we would have to give a short testimony of how we had come to faith. This was to take place in front of the church and friends.

In the weeks leading up to our baptism, my husband said to me that all the supernatural things kept happening to me and not him. I told him that he just needed to be real, to tell God how he was feeling, and ask God how to walk in the Spirit, and he would show him. So, we prayed together, and I asked the Holy Spirit to please make things more real for my husband. It was not long before that prayer was answered; in fact, it was the very next day that the Holy Spirit was to move in an amazing way.

My husband was at the print workshop, and it was while he was printing that he felt in his spirit a voice telling him to go back to his old house where he had lived as a young child. It would be a journey of about forty minutes. At first he ignored the voice, but it persisted, and he was asked again to go back to his old house. This time he stopped the printing machine, locked up the workshop, got in his car and began to drive to his old childhood home. On arriving at the house, he pulled up in the tree-lined lane, turned off the engine, and just sat there for a few minutes. He was trying to think of what he was going to say to whoever answered the door. God told me to come? No, he couldn't say that! After a few more minutes he decided he would just say he was in the area, and he used to live there.

So, he got out of his car and walked up the pathway leading to the house, when arriving at the door he realised there were now two bells; the house had been split into two flats. Not sure which bell to ring, he felt he should ring the top one, which he did, and a woman came down the stairs and answered the door.

One night I dreamed a dream.

As I was walking along the beach with my Lord.

Across the dark sky flashed scenes from my life.

For each scene, I noticed two sets of footprints in the sand,

One belonging to me and one to my Lord.

After the last scene of my life flashed before me

I looked back at the footprints in the sand.

I noticed that at many times along the path of my life,

especially at the very lowest and saddest times,

there was only one set of footprints.

'I don't understand why, when I need You most, You would leave me.'

He whispered, 'My precious child, I love you and will never leave you,

Never, ever, during your trials and testings.

When you saw only one set of footprints,

It was then that I carried you.'[10]

This had always reminded me of the night the Lord had shown me like a film part of my childhood, and had picked up the baby from the cot, and had carried me, never putting me down. That poem was such a beautiful illustration of God's love.

10. https://poem4today.com/footprints-poem.html. This version is attributed to Margaret Fishback Powers (1964) but there is some dispute over the original writer of this poem.

Chapter Three: Anointed for Service

Not very many weeks after we had been baptised, I was told about a conference that was going to be taking place in Birmingham, which was a long way from our home in the south of England.

One of my Christian friends was going and asked if I would like to go with her. It all sounded really exciting, but I really wasn't sure if I should or could go. I would be away for several nights and I had never left the children before; who could I ask to help my husband with the children? As only the girls would be at school, and I still had my son at home during the day, my husband would not be able to look after him at work. So, it really was not going to be a possibility.

My friend said, 'I will leave it with you, just pray about it.'

So I did pray. I said to the Lord, 'If I am meant to go, please would you make a way for me to go?'

The woman from my husband's old family home was coming to dinner that night, so we could meet each other; my husband had not seen her since their first meeting. I was delighted; she was lovely, and just as my husband had described her. She was really happy to hear about our baptism service. Our Christian landlords had even written a short article in their paper about my husband's experience before his baptism.

She then turned to me and asked me about my journey with the Lord; there was so much that had happened in the short time of my being a Christian, so I shared some of my story. I told her about the conference I had been invited to, and how I wasn't sure if I should go. She said she was going to that conference and yes, she felt the Lord was saying I should go, and he would make the way for me. She then said that she felt the Lord was saying he was going to anoint me, but that it would not be by the laying on of hands, he was going to do it sovereignly. Not sure what any of this meant, I thanked her and couldn't wait to see how the

Lord was going to make a way for me to go. As a really lovely evening came to an end, we said our goodbyes.

Within a few days of our new friend praying for me, the second confirmation came in a strange way. It was very early in the morning and my husband had gone to the Baptist church for a men's prayer meeting which was held once a week; men would get together and pray before going into work. At this prayer meeting was a man my husband had not met before; he was a pastor from another church.

After the meeting they had coffee and a croissant and a chat. The pastor was introduced to my husband, and they talked for a while about his recent baptism. The man was greatly encouraged by his story. My husband then said, 'You should meet my wife!' – meaning in the future! The man said, 'I want to meet her now.' Taken by surprise at his request, my husband remembers thinking for a minute about how I would feel about meeting a stranger at that early hour in the morning. After he had considered it, he answered the man, saying, 'OK, follow my car to our house – we only live a few minutes up the road.' So the man followed him home.

When my husband arrived at our house, I was a bit shocked to see he wasn't alone. I was getting the girls dressed and ready for school, as my husband was to be taking them in on his way to the print workshop. Once they were ready, my husband and the girls said their goodbyes to us and left.

Now with just my little son and this man, we sat down, and he started to ask me about my Christian life, my journey with God; it was a bit like an interview! I told him about the conference I was thinking about going to. He replied that I should go to the conference, and then started to say that he felt the Lord was saying to me, that I had been a Christian for thirteen years now and he wanted me to feed myself from the Word. He continued, explaining that I was no longer a 'baby' in Christ and that

God wanted to show me greater things for myself. I laughed, and said, 'I have only been a Christian just over thirteen months, not thirteen years!' But I received what he said and thanked him for coming.

This was so strange as not long before, a leader from my church had told me I was a baby in Christ and only needed the milk of the Word, and now this man was telling me I was not a baby any more. By being obedient to what my leader had said, I had been healed and was able to read my Bible out loud with confidence.

Once our visitor had left, and now encouraged that I should go to the conference in Birmingham, I remember turning to my little son and saying that now I just needed someone to look after him and his sisters if I was to go. This help came from someone in the church who said that she would love to look after my son during the day and take care of the girls after school until my husband got home. At last, I felt it was right to go to Birmingham; it had been confirmed by two people I had never met before, and the Lord had provided childcare.

The day that I was to leave for the conference in Birmingham had arrived at last. I had my bags packed and everything at home was organised. My friend came to collect me from the house. I was waved off by the children, and we started our four-hour journey to Birmingham. We were to stay with friends of my friend, who lived in the area. When we arrived at the house, I soon found that our hosts were not Christians and were quite sceptical about the conference we were to be attending.

The EuroFire conference was led by a German evangelist, Reinhard Bonnke.[11] He had led huge crusades in Africa, with hundreds of thousands of people coming to know Jesus and many miracles occurring – blind eyes were opened and the sick were healed. One of the things that struck me most about Reinhard was, although he was a great man of

---

11. He passed away in 2019.

God, he had such humility. How wonderful to come under his teaching and to hear about what God was doing in Africa.

That night we went to our first meeting; there was a great excitement and expectancy about the place. I had never been to such a large Christian meeting before. My friend and I soaked up every word that evening. I had such a desire to hear more about this amazing God.

That night, as I slept, I had a dream, and in my dream I saw a field of wheat. It was just blowing softly in the wind; then I saw a farmer on a tractor come and harvest the wheat. The next thing that I saw was a fire burning, but it was not consuming, it never changed in size or burned down. But I could not understand the meaning of my dream. The next morning at breakfast, as I drank my coffee, I told my friend what I had seen.

She said that the harvest fields were a symbol of people that didn't know Christ, and the farmer harvesting them was bringing them to salvation. I had never heard of non-Christians being referred to as harvest fields before.[12] But she could not explain the fire.

After breakfast we said goodbye to our hosts, and we would see them again in the evening.

We arrived at the conference centre for our next session.

That day, we went to a meeting where the speaker was sharing how a mother eagle sits on her nest high up on the mountain cliff edge, feeding her offspring until they can fly and feed themselves. When they are ready, she stirs up the nest and throws them out; if they start to fall, she swoops down and scoops them up and does it all over again until the fledglings imitate her, and spread their wings and fly.

Suddenly the words that the man that my husband had brought back from the men's prayer meeting made sense to me. I knew what God was saying to me. He was wanting to teach me to fly, to be in the Spirit

12. Matthew 9:37-38.

and to be led by him and to listen more closely to his voice. And he was teaching me to feed myself. I was no longer a baby; it was time for me to spread my wings.

After that meeting, I remember talking to one of the many people who were there as part of the ministry team for the conference. I shared with the woman about the dream I had the night before, and how I could not understand what the fire was. She said I should read about Moses as it sounded like the burning bush in Exodus 3. She said God was wanting to speak to me and that I needed to find out what he wanted to tell me. I thanked her for her help, and said I would seek God for myself and find out what it was he was saying. I then went to a meeting led by intercessor Suzette Hattingh on prayer before the evening session to put into practise what I had learned earlier that day. I also remember at one of her workshops we had to pray for healing. Several of us prayed for a lady who had a painful arm injury. Suzette called from the stage to 'check your healing' but the woman whimpered in pain.

I said, 'Lord, I don't understand why she isn't healed.' The Lord said, 'She is, but she is afraid to move her arm. Come against the fear, bind the spirit of fear and loose her.'[13] So, just as the Lord had said, I did. I then said to her, 'Try again and move your arm.' And this time she did. She raised it right up in the air and started shouting, 'I'm healed! Praise God, praise God! I am healed.'

I had seen my first miracle where I had prayed for someone for healing. The Lord had told me what to do, and as I did what he told me to do, there was a miracle. I was greatly encouraged by Suzette's meetings on how to be led effectively by the spirit.

I couldn't wait for the next day!

The following day in one of Reinhard's meetings, he said that he wanted to pray for people who could not hear the voice of God. He

13. Matthew 18:18.

asked those people to stand up so he could pray for them and almost everybody stood. I felt very self-conscious still sitting down, so I said to the Lord, 'I can hear your voice, but I will stand up, as the people around me were making me feel uncomfortable.' I then said, 'Lord, I acknowledge that I can hear you, but would you please sharpen my hearing to your voice?'

During the conference, I was learning to listen closely to the leading of the Holy Spirit. He was showing me that God had given me a ministry, and during this time, he was equipping me for the task ahead. I had learned if I just stepped out and did whatever he asked me to do, it would be successful. I just had to follow his leading, and not do what I thought. It was very exciting.

I remember meeting a woman in the corridor and God told me to say; 'Wasn't it wonderful that we can go directly into the Lord's presence?' She didn't think that we could. She went on to tell me that she was a Roman Catholic, and that she could only go to God through her priest. I replied that Jesus was the great high priest[14] and when he died on the cross, the curtain was torn in two,[15] and that he had made the way open to God. She was rejoicing because this was a revelation to her, news that she needed to hear. But what she didn't know was that the things I was telling her were from the scripture that I had read. I had read these things, but the Lord had put them in my mouth. The Holy Spirit knew what she needed to hear and, on my part, gave me the words to say. This was great; all I had to do was be obedient to his leading and I could trust the Lord for the words. It was to be a great adventure!

'Who do you want me to speak to next, Lord?' I enquired.

The Lord said, 'See the man over there? He oversees the finances for Reinhard's ministry.'

14. Hebrews 4:14-16.

15. Matthew 27:51.

I had seen him on the platform with Reinhard before. 'I want you to give him all your money and tell him to put it into Africa.'

I had taken £100 with me to buy food and give to our hosts, but they had not wanted to take anything from us. I said, 'Lord, I had wanted to buy a couple of worship tapes to take home.' I wasn't even spending money on food; I hadn't realised at the time that I was fasting. I was so full of God, and I just had a different kind of hunger. So I went over to the man and told him that the Lord had asked me to put this money into Reinhard's ministry in Africa. He assured me that he would.

I then met an African man. We shook hands and exchanged just a few words. I said, 'Isn't God wonderful!'

He replied, 'Your hand is on fire. You are on fire. We need you in Africa!'

I laughed and walked on.

The conference was coming to an end; I had learned so much about prayer and about being led by the Spirit. I think I was being equipped for what God wanted for my life.

On one of the last evenings, we invited our hosts to come to the meeting. The wife said that she would come. It was to be a good session for her to attend, as a woman who had been in a wheelchair and had been suffering from numerous ailments came to give her testimony about how, at a revival meeting earlier in the year, Reinhard had prayed for her healing, and she had been healed. She was a Sunday school teacher, and one of the children in her class had a dream; the child had told her that God was going to heal her. She went to the revival meeting and was miraculously healed.

That night, after the meeting, my friend and I drove back to the house. All the way home, my friend kept saying to me, 'We have got to speak to our hosts. We need to lead them to the Lord.'

I asked the Lord what to do, and would he give me the words to speak to our host, the wife, who had been at the conference? But to my surprise the Holy Spirit told me not to speak to her. I told my friend what the Lord had said to me; she just said that I could not have heard from the Lord.

When we got back to the house, we waited a further hour for our host to return home. When she eventually turned up, we asked her what had happened, why she was so late in getting back. She replied, a little agitated, that she had got lost and had been on her way to Coventry. This was crazy, I thought. She knew her way around locally. I think she had even worked at the conference centre at some point. But it wasn't crazy at all; the Lord had sent her to Coventry! When you send someone to Coventry, it means you don't speak to them. This was confirmation of what the Holy Spirit had told me.

I said goodnight and went to bed. My friend continued talking to our host late into the night about the meeting, which our host said she had not enjoyed. So being led by the Spirit wasn't just talking when God wanted you to, but also not speaking. God's timing is always perfect.

The final evening at the conference was the night that God anointed me. This was the night that had been spoken about two weeks earlier, when the woman from my husband's old house had come to meet me. God was going to anoint me, but it was going to be sovereign, not by the laying on of hands – which was the only way I had ever seen people prayed for.

Earlier that day, I had found time to be alone with the Lord and he had shown me a picture of a field. Around the field were ditches, but there was no water in them. I didn't really understand the picture, but this was about to change.

Reinhard led the final meeting. He said that God was wanting to anoint people who knew they were being called to be Holy Spirit-led evangelists. He then said he would lay hands on them to receive their anointing. He started to call people forward, country by country, finishing with England. People queued for what seemed like hours. I went outside for a while to be alone with God, as I knew it wouldn't be by the laying on of hands that I was to be anointed.

Who should come up to me but Suzette! She said: 'Why are you out here? Go in and receive your anointing.' So, I went back and joined the huge queues. While standing in a long line, I remembered the field I had been shown that morning with the empty ditches. And then, right next to me as I stood in the queue, was a printed sign, that read PUSH BAR.

I suddenly understood. To allow the water to flow, I needed to push the bar in the Spirit, it would be released like a floodgate and the water would flow around the fields. So, in the Spirit, in my mind, I pushed the bar and water just rushed out, flowing like a river filling the empty ditches.

The next thing that happened was Reinhard called from the platform, 'I will not lay hands on anyone else, but I want you all to get into a long line and hold hands and I will pray. It will be like a river flowing and the river will anoint you.' So, we all joined hands; just as he said, the power of God ran from person to person, just like the water that had been released as the floodgate bar was pushed.

It was a bit like a domino effect. One person after another just fell to the ground as the power hit them in this long line. I don't know how long we stayed on the floor, but when I stood up, I knew that God had anointed me with the ministry he had placed in my hands during the 'Reflections around the cross' time in the Baptist church.

Before leaving the centre, my friend had bought a lot of Christian tapes to take home, and she handed me two, saying, 'These are for you, a present.' They were the tapes I had really wanted, unknown to her, the very two worship tapes I had mentioned to the Lord!

teThis had been such an adventure in God: I had been anointed for
service, learned so much about prayer, was not a baby in Christ now,
and was to feed myself from the Word. God had sent two people I did
not know leading up to the conference into my life, telling me what God
was going to do. And it had all come to pass.

The next day we packed our belongings into the car. We had promised
to give a lift to someone who lived on our way home. My friend was
still very disappointed that we had not led our hosts to the Lord. I was
the last one out of the house as we were leaving, I turned to my hosts,
thanked them for their kind hospitality, and the wife turned to me and
said she would look me up if ever she was in our area – if I wasn't in
Africa! We both laughed. Then I said my goodbyes to her husband. They
waved us off as we pulled out of the drive.

We had been driving for less than an hour when I said to my friend,
'I have such a strong desire to pray for the husband. Is it possible to pull
over somewhere?' She pulled up into a lay-by, I got out of the car, and
the strangest thing happened. I started to cry. I felt this terrible burden
to pray for this man. The Lord had shown me he was dying; that he
didn't have long to live. The crying was from my heart, it was a deep pain
I had never experienced before. I remember saying to the Lord, 'I will
pray for his healing.' The Lord said that if he were healed, he would die
spiritually, and to pray for his salvation.

I then did as the Lord had said and prayed for his salvation. As I did
this, the sheer anguish and pain left me. The Lord had shown me he
would die physically, but not spiritually. He would know Christ before
he died and would have eternal life. With that I got back into the car and
told the others what had happened.

I realised that it was travail, which we had learned about in one of
the sessions on prayer with Suzette. Travail is like when a woman is in
labour, there is pain until the birth. It is the same with prayer; until

r45

we have prayed it though, given birth in the Spirit, we won't see the results. Once we pray it through, the pain leaves. This was another new experience for me.

Not far now, and we would be at the house of the young woman to whom we had given a lift. The Holy Spirit had given something for me to say to her. At the time of giving her the word, she said it wasn't right. But now she started to cry, saying the things I had previously said to her were true and she wanted me to pray for her. I agreed that I would once we arrived at her destination.

This was another thing that the Lord had taught me – not always, when we give a word that we believe is from him to the person we believe it's for, would it be accepted straight away.

At last, we reached my house, pulling into the road where I lived. I turned to my friend and thanked her for taking me to the conference, it had been such an amazing adventure in God. I then hurriedly grabbed my bag from the back seat. I got out and literally ran up the path to the front door, so excited to be home with my family. The door opened. I was greeted by my husband and three very excited children, who all seemed to have got colds in my absence. I remember saying, 'We won't have colds in this house!' and bound the spirit of infirmity and laughed.

It was so lovely to be home. The children told me they had a surprise for me, that it was in the playroom, and I needed to close my eyes. They led me into the playroom, then all shouted at once, 'You can open them now!' I opened my eyes and there was a beautiful, fluffy, champagne-coloured Persian kitten which was placed into my hands. They had named him Sebastian and he was beautiful. We had been begging my husband for weeks to let us have a kitten, and he had given in and wanted to surprise me. The only problem was that while I was away, the Lord had said to me that we would be travelling, so having pets would not have been an option. I didn't say anything to the family, and just cuddled the kitten, which was gorgeous.

Evening came, and we sat down to have a short prayer time before the children went to bed. We would go round each of the children asking them to pray; the two older ones were now four and five. When it came to my four-year-old daughter, she would always say the same prayer. 'Thank you, Jesus, for a lovely day.' But this time she prayed, 'Thank you, Lord, for giving Mummy the keys.' Then she giggled. She didn't know or understand what she had just said. But of course, I did. The scripture that came to mind was in Matthew 16:19: 'I will give you the keys of the kingdom of heaven; whatever you bind on earth will be bound in heaven, and whatever you loose on earth will be loosed in heaven.' The Lord had taught me so much on prayer, and how to pray in the authority he had given me as a Christian; how to pray in his name. He had given me the keys.

The conference had been such a wonderful time in God. I remember thinking to myself, nothing could ever come close to what I had experienced in God. I prayed, 'Lord, you have my heart, and I want to give you the whole of my life. I want to be the person you have called me to be. I want to serve you for the rest of my life. I love to be in your presence; life with you is such an adventure. Nothing could ever compare with it.' And finally I said, 'Don't ever take your Holy Spirit from me.'[16]

Not long after this, I started to put into practice all that I had learned at the conference. The Baptist church we were attending was to have a mission, an outreach on the beach with another Baptist church on the coast. We decided we would go.

Arriving at the beach location, we all jumped out of the car and headed towards the green where there was a platform. We could hear people singing the songs that we sang in church. As we approached, we saw people from our church. The pastor was on the platform. The children, excited about being at the beach, asked my husband if he

---

16. Psalm 51:11.

would take then down to the sands, which he seemed pleased to be able to do. He met up with a friend, another father from church, who was also heading down to the sea.

I went up towards the platform. Our pastor was just starting to preach. I looked around, and it seemed it was mostly people from our church and the other church standing around to listen, and a few were giving out printed tracts. I began to pray. I had asked the Lord if he could please give me someone he wanted me to talk to, like he had done at the conference, and I knew he would give me the words to speak.

I felt that I should walk away from the green and up on to the promenade. It was a beautiful, hot sunny day; the sun was glistening on the water. I could hear the sound of the gulls. The children were playing on the sand. I could smell the salt in the air. What a wonderful day to be there. Up on the promenade, I could see two women walking towards me. I asked the Lord, was I to speak to them? 'Yes,' came the reply. So, I approached them and said what a lovely day it was, to which they both agreed. I then said, 'You're probably wondering what is going on down there!' Looking towards the green, I started to share with them how I became a Christian not that long ago, and how we could have a relationship with this loving God. I shared some of the exciting things that had happened since becoming a Christian, how real God was, how life with him was an adventure and if they wanted to know God and wanted it to be real for them, I would pray for them. They said they did and asked me to pray. I prayed with them both and they asked Jesus into their hearts.

I then invited them to come and meet my pastor, where they could give their details and he would come and visit them. But it was decided that the pastor from the other church would visit them as they lived nearer to his church. I never saw them again and I always wondered what would happen to them if they didn't get the same faith teaching I'd had. But the Holy Spirit told me if they really wanted to know him, he would reveal himself to them, just as he had and was still doing in my life.

I was learning that you play your part in leading someone to him, and others would do their part. I always found this hard. But the Holy Spirit reminded me again, if you really want to know Jesus and live this life, he will show you great things and take you on great adventures in him, as he knows our lives, where we have come from and how to fix us.

That summer, we took a family holiday at a Christian hotel/holiday camp. We had been told about a Christian hotel in Kent by someone at church. We thought it would be a great opportunity for us to have a holiday away. It was near a beach, and it also had a swimming pool at the hotel. We had never been to anything like this before, so we didn't really know what to expect. We were all excited to be going on holiday, and was this to be another adventure in God?

On arriving at the hotel, we checked into our room, which was a big family room where we would all sleep. Then we went to check out the rest of the facilities; there were lovely grounds with a pool. In the hotel was a Christian bookshop. There was a dining room where we were to have all our meals; we would be seated at large tables with other guests. So, we got to meet a lot of Christians from all sorts of church backgrounds. While we were there, the Lord gave me many people to pray for. I was still putting into practice all that I had learned at the Birmingham conference. Some people wanted to be baptised in the Holy Spirit, and to speak an unlearned language. There were lots of different needs. I think there would normally be a visiting minister who would have an evening meeting, but not while we were there. Anyway, God used me to pray with people; word soon got around, and people would just come and ask for prayer.

During one of the days there, the Lord told me that he wanted me to write to the couple I had stayed with in Birmingham. Just before we had gone on holiday, I'd had a phone call from my friend with whom I had gone to Birmingham. She had been phoned by our hosts, who told her that they were having to move house for various reasons, and they would not be able to buy a house of the same calibre. My friend asked if I would pray for them. And now, weeks after the Lord had told me not to speak to the wife of that couple, he was now telling me it was the right time. But what did he want me to say? So, I started to pray.

I went to the bookshop in the hotel and bought some headed notepaper. At the top of the page was a small picture of praying hands and a scripture, Jeremiah 33:3. It read: 'Call to me and I will answer'. So, I began to write the letter as the Holy Spirit led me. I told the couple that I was sorry to hear their news, but that I was sure God was going to help them find a house and that I was praying for them at this difficult time. A few months later, I was to get a very excited phone call from our hosts in Birmingham. My friend had passed on my number, as the couple had wanted to relay the news to me personally. The wife told me that they had bought a beautiful house, it was the same calibre as their old home, and they had got it at a lower price as the vendors wanted a quick sale. She then went on to say that when they first went to the house, she saw a plaque up on the wall; it was praying hands, just like the one on the notepaper! She said she knew the house was theirs. Wasn't God good! Then she finally told me that the vendors had had a beautiful coach lamp up outside but had taken it when they left. I then told her they must have been Christians, and that as Christians, light was a symbol: Jesus is the 'light of the world' (John 8:12). They had taken the light, but she needed to bring the light into her life; she needed Jesus. She needed to get her own coach lamp.

This was very exciting to me as the Lord had shown me that he has a perfect time for everything. He knew that later, she would be open and ready to hear the word.

Seasons were coming and going. I love the summer, a time when the roses are in full bloom, and all the coloured shrubs put on their display, one after another. The apple tree was laden with growing fruit, and the allotment bursting with produce, with the hens enjoying their dust baths. It was a busy time for nature, and for us.

I was pregnant with our fourth child, and I was filled with a deep love for this little life within.

The long summer holidays were here, so entertaining the children was my main priority, with hours of fun at the beach or at my parents' farm, where the children would enjoy feeding the animals or playing at the edge of the duck pond, scrapping the clay mud with their hands, then moulding it into pots and drying them in the sun.

The print workshop was a hive of activity, the printing machine now working longer into the night. Often my husband would be home late. We would also go to meetings such as house group, Full Gospel Business Men's meetings, and on Monday night, we took part in outreach in Brighton, so life was hectic.

I remember one evening, I had a phone call from my husband saying he needed to stay late at the workshop, as he had a man coming to look at the printing machine. Something was wrong with it. I was very tired; it had been a very long day with the children, and I was really upset as he seemed to be home later and later. I remember saying to him that I wouldn't cook supper or even tidy up the children's toys as I was so cross. I put the phone down.

The children were all asleep in bed. I went and sat in the sitting room and started to cry. I felt really unloved, I couldn't explain it, just alone, as I was now spending so many evenings on my own. I asked the Lord if he could send someone round as I really needed to talk about how I was feeling. I even asked if he could please send our pastor. But I knew he would never be able to come as he was very busy and had never been to our house before. I heard something being dropped through our letter box. I went to have a look; it was the weekly property newspaper. I picked it up and sat down, and as I did, the strangest thing happened. From feeling really unloved, upset and cross, I suddenly felt the most incredible peace come over me. It was like Jesus had just walked into the room. I opened the paper and looked at the houses. I remember saying to the Lord, a bit like a child, 'If we had a bigger house, everything would be all right.' Our house was getting too small for us, especially now that another baby was on the way. I didn't really know how to fix the way I was feeling.

I turned to the paper and printed in big letters was an advertisement that filled the page.

NOW WE ARE TOGETHER, ANYTHING IS POSSIBLE

I knew the Lord was talking to me. I was not alone; I had him, he was not going anywhere, and with him anything was possible. His peace really does '[transcend] all understanding' (Philippians 4:7). Then I asked the Lord, could he please keep my husband at work a bit longer so I would have time to cook a meal and tidy the toys away? I cooked his favourite meal and put candles on the table. I had also cut out the words from the newspaper and stuck them up on the fridge door.

My husband arrived home; he would have been expecting me to have been upset, toys everywhere and no meal. But he was greeted with a smile, and to his surprise his favourite meal on the table and no toys to be seen. He kissed me and apologised for being so late. He then said, 'I know God has done something here.'

I told him all that had happened, how I was so upset and had asked God for our pastor to come round. I then showed him the cutting on the fridge door. I told him how it was almost as if Jesus had walked into the room, and the most amazing peace I felt.

Just as we finished our meal there was a knock at the door. Who would be calling at this time of night? My husband went to the door and in walked our pastor! He said he was visiting our neighbours on church business and thought he would call in.

I just laughed. I said, 'You are too late!' I told him the whole story. I said that the Lord had come instead, but also thanked him for coming. I then showed him the newspaper cutting on the fridge door.

Our pastor said he knew God was doing something in our lives. He didn't want to intervene. He said that he knew the Lord had something special for us to do, then he left.

It wasn't very many weeks after that evening that my husband decided that we were to make the thirty-minute journey to Brighton each week for church; he felt that we were going there on a Monday night already, for outreach, and that we were to cut out our house group.

We still went to the Full Gospel Business Men's meetings, which allowed wives to come sometimes. It was on one of those occasions that I had gone along to watch a video about faith and healing. We were a small group – the leader's wife and I the only women and about five men in all. We watched the video and I felt faith rise up in me. After the video finished, the leader of the group asked if anyone would like prayer for healing, and a man said that he would like to be prayed for. The leader of the group asked if anyone would like to pray for him. I said that I would like to. I asked him what it was that he needed prayer for. I could see he had a light bandage on his hand. He held his hand out towards me and told me he had shingles. I had never heard of shingles before.

I began to pray. I didn't think that much had happened. I asked the Holy Spirit what to do, and he said, 'Bind the spirit of fear!' as that was the root of his problem. As I prayed for him binding the spirit of fear and loosing him, I accidentally hit his hand, not hard. It made him jump and the fear left him. He then went on to tell me that his mother was coming to visit him and he got very stressed about her visits. We gave him a lift home as he was unable to drive. On the journey, he said that he was so encouraged that God had used me to pray for him, knowing the short time that I had been a Christian. He went on to say that he had been a Christian for thirty years and was longing for more of God. I learned that the next day he had gone back to the doctor and was allowed back to work, after being off sick.

That evening was to show us that just by watching a video faith would come, and we realised that there were a lot of very hungry Christians who wanted more of God.

So that's when my husband and I decided to have a video evening at our house once a week and have a time of ministry afterwards. Those evenings were to grow and grow; we sometimes had as many as twenty hungry Christians in our sitting room. And the times of ministry, which we held in the children's playroom, would often go on long into the night. One night three people got baptised in the Holy Spirit at the same time. We would pray into people lives, and see people come to Christ. Even during the week we would have people knock on the door and want prayer, mostly to be baptised in the Holy Spirit. It was exciting as word got around about the ministry times.

So, by moving to the church in Brighton, we had cut out our old weekly meetings, but we were now filling the evenings that my husband was home with new groups that would meet in our house. We had even printed our own little tract with a short summary of our testimonies and put a PO box number on the back, so people could make contact that way. One woman who had picked up the tract had written to us but had put the wrong PO box number on it, so it was a few months later before I was able to contact her.

I had arranged to meet her in town and have coffee. I was in the last months of my pregnancy by that time. On arriving at the coffee shop, I saw a young woman sitting alone. The Lord told me it was her, so I introduced myself. She looked tired, as if life had been hard for her. She went on to tell me she had been working in a care home, doing night shifts. She had asked the Lord for help because she had a drink problem. She had read our tract and prayed. During the night, she felt that something had happened, and that God had met with her. Afterwards, she had not had another drink and had left the care home and got a new job. She had realised that she was an alcoholic and had joined an AA group. She was so pleased that I had made contact.

I talked to her about the Lord and how we were meant to meet. I was so sorry that it had been months, rather than days later, but I was delighted to hear how the Lord had taken care of her. How he had revealed himself to her, and her need of him. So that day, we prayed together, and she asked Jesus into her heart. I then arranged for her to come to our home and gave her some literature. She then joined us weekly to go to Brighton for the Monday night meetings, and also came with us to church on Sundays. I had started a small group with new believers, people I had led to the Lord. I saw this lady's countenance change from someone whose life had been hard to a beautiful young woman who had life in Jesus. She had a radiant smile and even her hair shone! She shared later that she used to sleep rough. It was so wonderful to see how God had reached down and taken a broken life that had reached rock bottom, and lovingly lifted her up and given her new life in him.

Christmas was the time of year when we would have end-of-term nativity plays, carols, Christmas parties and endless mince pies. Also, the evenings would be getting darker earlier. I always remember the shrieks of delight coming from the children, as they would see the twinkly lights on the decorated Christmas trees in the windows of the houses as we drove home from school.

There was great excitement in the air as the children counted down the days on their advent calendars, during the run-up to Christmas. I can see, as I look back, the children wrapping their little presents, the coloured paper and so much Sellotape it would have taken an age to open! They would usually give one of their own possessions to each other, a half-used pack of crayons, or a well-worn toy, but always with love. My second daughter's birthday was also on Christmas day! But the children knew that this was the time of year that we also celebrated the birth of Christ. I would always have to explain the baby in the nativity manger grew up into the man Jesus, found in their children's Bible. It did, however, take a little while for the younger ones to grasp that concept. And I, too, was due to have another baby on Christmas day, my first baby as a Christian. I asked the Lord if I could please have the baby before or after Christmas, as I didn't want two of my children to have the same birthday.

I went into labour on Christmas eve, 1989. The Lord even provided me with a Christian nurse who safely delivered our beautiful daughter. She was perfect in every way, and she completed our family. We marked the occasion with a picture of the children with their new baby sister. We had the scripture printed under it from Psalm 139:13-14: 'For you created my inmost being; you knit me together in my mother's womb. I praise you because I am fearfully and wonderfully made'.

And she really was.

After the birth of our beautiful daughter, I was really very tired, juggling family life, four young children, two just at school, one at nursery, and a new baby. And all our Christian commitments, and still going into the print workshop.

The Monday nights were coming to an end as the pastor was planning to live in America. The pastor who would eventually run the church now took over the new believers' group. This was done to take some of the pressure off me, so I could rest. However, we still did the video evenings, but now only once a fortnight.

Chapter Four: My Deliverer and Protection

One Monday, I was driving down to the print workshop with our baby daughter as my husband had needed me to come in and answer the phone while he was to visit a customer. While I was driving, I suddenly began to think about my grandmother, who had died when I was just a baby, I didn't really remember her, I only knew about her through the things I had been told. Apparently she had done a thing called 'table tapping' where someone puts letters out on a table and calls upon the dead.

'How strange,' I thought, 'to be thinking about someone I don't even remember.' When I arrived at the workshop my husband had already left, so I went into the office with my now sleeping baby. I sat down in the office chair and as I did, I began to cry. I was so upset that my grandmother had done this table tapping. I was saying to the Lord that I was sorry for her involvement in the occult.

Then I remembered a time in my own life when I had been given, as a young teenager, a pack of Tarot cards, and how at school one evening we had got them out, but I didn't know how to read them. I just remember becoming really frightened and putting them away. Then I took them down to the bottom off our garden, where the bonfires were lit, and I burned them. Afterwards, I placed a cross on them made out of two little twigs.

How did I know to do that? I don't know. It was amazing, the Lord knew me, even then. So, I remember praying and asking the Lord to forgive me for that time at school, and as I did, I felt the burden lift.

Sometime later my husband came back. When I got home, I called a friend of mine who I know was an intercessor for the church and would have been praying for the Monday night meeting, which we would be attending later. I told what had happened, how I had been thinking of a grandmother I didn't really know about the table tapping.

The babysitter arrived and we left for the Monday night meeting. At the meeting we worshipped and sang about the blood of Jesus and the power in it. The pastor said that there were people that had done something occult as children and had got frightened, and that the Lord wanted to set them free.

As I stood there I shook from head to foot. I knew that I was one of those children. Even though nothing had happened to me physically, spiritually I had opened a door. And from that day at school, I had become afraid of anything to do with the occult. I went forward with other people, and we were all wonderfully set free. This was yet another side of my wonderful God. He had shown me my grandmother's sin and had set me free from the curses, and had led me to repentance for when I was a child and had unwittingly opened the door to the occult. A friend recommended a good book for me to read after I had told them about what had happened to me.[17]

Another side to my amazing God was when he was to show himself as our protector. In the summer of 1990, one beautiful July evening, my husband and I were going to dinner at the home of friends, who lived the other side of Brighton. We were going to watch football with them; they were both were avid football fans, we were not, so it would be a new experience for us. It was a match between England and Germany. We had taken the baby with us, as she was still able to fit her carrycot, and our hosts loved babies, especially this one!

We all sat down to have our meal in the little sitting room, all decorated with flags and football-related bits. They had gone to a lot of trouble; the atmosphere was great, I could feel it, and it was contagious. We were

17. Neil T. Anderson, *The Steps to Freedom in Christ* (Bloomington, MN: Bethany House, 2017

well and truly caught up in it. I was starting to feel really excited. We sat down to watch the match, we all shouted at the screen, cheering England on. We had really enjoyed our evening with our friends and our new experience of football but were aware that we needed to get home for the babysitter, so we placed the baby in her carrycot on the back seat of the car and set off.

For some reason, my husband must have taken a wrong turning and ended up going through Brighton instead of the by-pass round it.

We were just about to drive up a road, when a tall man dressed in a suit came out from nowhere and stepped in front of our car. It made us jump so we stopped and wound down the window to speak to the man, who told us that there was rioting going on in the road we were about to enter. England fans were smashing shop windows and throwing rocks through car windows. We were in a German car, a VW Passat. This most certainly would have been a target. My husband thanked the man for his help, and hastily turned the car around and drove on. We didn't see any of the commotion he had warned us about. I remember commenting on how out of place this tall man looked in his smart suit late at night in the middle of Brighton.

The next day on the news, we heard how England fans in Brighton had smashed windows in the area we had been approaching. Had this tall man not stepped out to stop us, things could have been very different. We always wondered if in fact the man was an angel.

Another night comes to mind. My husband had called me from the print workshop saying he would be home late again as he was going to Brighton to see a friend from church. He had just got a new car and was wanting to show it to him. He then said he was 'going out with the lads', as he put it. I was not very pleased. I remember the same feeling of being unloved come over me that I had felt before, and I remember thanking the Lord for his love and being with me, never leaving me alone.

It was starting to get late, and my husband still wasn't home. I was sitting down reading my Bible, praying, and as I did, I saw a fire and I felt my husband was in danger. Then I heard a voice saying, 'Let him go through the fire; let him be tried and tested.' But instead I prayed, 'Lord, please protect my husband, please let him get home safely!'

A short time later my husband pulled up into the drive and came into the house. He told me that on the way home, he had been driving really fast, when he had seen what he thought was a bonfire in the distance in the fields; he had narrowly avoided being in a car accident where the cars were on fire. He said that he felt that the Lord had said to him, 'How much longer will you mess around?' and that he needed to get serious about the call on our lives.

I then told him what had happened, how I had just been praying and had seen the fire and prayed protection over him around the same time.

I think that was a turning point for my husband. From that time on, he became really serious about the call on our lives, and started to look for a Bible school. He even went to America to check out the ministry school that was associated with our church. But it he said it was not the school for us. It was to be a few months after he had been to America that I was handed a Christian newspaper from South Africa. It was a paper from a church called the Rhema, and in this paper, I read that they had a Bible school; there was a two-year course. I realised that the pastor was one of the preachers from the Birmingham conference. I had heard him preach and wondered if this was the Bible school for us.

My husband said that we should apply, and if it was the right place, God would show us. Life went on as normal, we continued our video evenings, but church was changing. The time had come for the pastor who had led the Monday night meetings to leave with his family to live in America, and the pastor that had been filling in part-time was now to take over the church on Sundays.

The reply from South Africa had finally arrived; we had been accepted on the two-year course at the Bible school. We were so excited, but it was also very daunting, the thought of moving country with a young family. There was so much that need to be sorted out before we could go. We would need to rent out our house while we were away. My husband thought that he would put the printing business up for sale as he didn't feel he would be printing again, and we would need an income to support us while in South Africa. And so, it was the business now up for sale, and we asked an agent to value the house for rental. I remember when they came round, they asked lots of questions on the type of tenant we wanted – would we allow pets, a family, people out at work, professionals?

I said, 'Doctors!' The agent laughed and said that working doctors would not be renting and student doctors were provided with accommodation at the hospital.

We agreed that once we had sold our business and were ready to go, we would be in touch. It was not long before the business was sold. We got in touch with the rental agency who then found us tenants. It just so happened they were doctors who did not want to be in hospital accommodation, as they had two cats! We agreed that they could have their cats at the house. We didn't mind too much as we ourselves had had a beautiful Persian kitten, which we had sadly had to re-home as one of the children was allergic to its hair. It was to be a six-month let to begin with. And in our absence, if the agent was happy with the tenants, they would renew the tenancy. As we were due to start Bible school in less than three months, we decided to rent a house. It meant we had time to sell our cars, pack up the house and for the sale of our printing company to go through. So, we left our house, all packed up with just our suitcases, the baby's buggy, and belongings that we would take to Africa. We stayed in a terraced house, backing onto the railway, next door to a small church hall.

The house was damp, dark, with bright-red carpets and the dye would come off on the children's clothing. It was so different from our home we had just left. But we would encourage ourselves by saying it was only temporary, just until the sale of the business went though, then we would be off to Africa. We sold our cars and drove round in an old vehicle which had been lent to us by someone from church. I think most people thought that we had lost all our money and probably felt sorry for us. I could see them talking at the school gates, and then stop as I approached. It was really humbling.

I remember one day, while at home in our new surroundings, I said to the Lord, 'I told you you could have everything all those months ago after the conference in Birmingham!' I still meant it – I wanted to go to Africa. I wanted to serve him and to live in the fullness of his life. There was still nothing this world could offer compared to the life I had found in him. The tears were running down my face, but I knew that I meant it.

This was to be tested. A beautiful Georgian House came up for sale just around the corner from the girls' school, near the church where I had started my Christian journey. It was the house that I had always wanted to own one day; it was perfect, we could have had Christian meetings there in the two big sitting rooms. There was even premises at the back of the house in another building, in which we could have housed our printing business; my husband found out that we could get permission to run the business from there. And it even had a little flat we could let out to help with the mortgage. It was perfect in every way. We worked out that it would be possible to buy it. But we knew this was not the plan; we were going to Africa.

The man buying the business was dragging it on and on, and as the time got closer, he wanted it at a reduced price. We decided that we would not agree, and he pulled out of the sale. So here we were, still in England with a few weeks to go before the start of Bible school, no business sale and tenants in our house. We decided to move house as we knew that we would now not be going to Bible school until the following year. So, we found a holiday home that we could rent for the next three months, until we could return home. It was luxury. It was on the sea front in a nearby town; a flat with the beach as a garden for the children.

The children loved it there; so did we. We would spend hours collecting shells, painting pebbles and playing in the rockpools. We could even hear the sound of the waves from the open window and every morning ducks from the local park would come, leaving the lake for their breakfast. The children would eagerly await their arrival at the patio doors of our ground-floor flat when we would suddenly hear a thud as the ducks landed and a terrible commotion, quacking for their food. When completely full and they could eat no more, they would fly back to their home in the park. This was a really lovely place to be; it helped soften the disappointment of not going to Africa for another year.

We gave back the car we had borrowed and got a new car. We were settled into our new life on the beach, and would be returning to our house soon. After the three months were up, we returned home and got back into the rhythm of normal life. We were full of expectancy in the year leading up to the move to South Africa; this time we would have time to get it right. But I don't think it was so much getting it wrong, but the timing.

I then started to think a lot about being dyslexic. How would I be able to manage with all the written work on the course? I was beginning to think of my days at school, when I would feel I was stupid. And here I was as an adult, putting myself back into a classroom environment. I knew that this time would be different because I wasn't alone, the Bible was alive to me now and I knew the Holy Spirit was my teacher; I longed so much to be saturated in his Word.

But it wasn't that, it was the memories of my childhood in the classroom that haunted me. My sisters and I had started a new school together as our old school had closed. I was seven at the time. We were all put into different classes, but I was put down a year, now in a classroom with my sister who was thirteen months younger. I didn't mind that so much, it was more the fact that she could do all the work better than I could. I struggled my way through the years at the junior school, enjoying art, pottery, sport, anything that didn't involve the written word. At the age of eleven I was to leave the junior school; my sister was amazing at ballet, and had got a place in one of the top ballet schools in the country, where she was to board. The head teacher met with my parents and said that it would not be in my best interest to proceed to the senior school, as it would be too academic for me, and they should look for a new school. My parents found a place that was just the kind of school the head teacher had described. It was a day and boarding school.

I started off as a day girl going on the train into school, with some older girls to keep an eye on me. I would then meet my best friend at the next stop, where I would make the rest of the journey, and after disembarking, we would walk the rest of the way to school, stopping off at the sweet shop.

When I first started the school, I remember thinking it was so old-fashioned it was like it was going back in time. It had been started by the current head mistress, who was now a very old lady. She still had virtually the same staff running the school, with of course a few new teachers coming and going. Even the original cook was still there. We had the same every week; the worst was tapioca on Wednesday. We called it frog spawn! I was lucky to have a friend who loved it and we would swap bowls after she had eaten hers. We had old-fashioned desks with inkwells, and the teacher would be sitting at a tall desk in front of the class, very different from the modern school I had just come from.

I remember my first week, being asked to come up to the teacher's desk and read aloud a passage in front of the class, as I had watched my peers do. I remember just standing there. I was frozen to the spot with tears running down my face. The teacher asked me to compose myself, then much to my relief allowed me to go back to my desk and sit down. My peers were mostly kind, but there would be those who would mock me, saying, 'Didn't your old school teach you to read?'

As I started to make new friends and settle into life at school, I became a boarder. There was one advantage to this school being run by old ladies; their eyesight wasn't very good so there was always lots of note-passing going on in class. We would make ink bombs out of blotting paper dipped into our inkwells and see who could flick them the furthest. I think I became a bit of a class clown. We were tested each week on what we had learned, and instead of the teacher marking our paper, we passed it to the girl next to us for them to mark as the answers were read out. My friend would ask me what mark I wanted out of ten and I would say seven; I probably really only got three or four. This went on all through my time at that school; the only real problem was end-of-term exams! My poor results were put down to exam nerves. I had learned to wear a mask; only I really knew what I could and could not do – and, of course, my friend marking my paper!

We had a few younger teachers who would mark our work, and one who was very kind got me a spelling book so I could learn spellings; she was the only teacher who ever seemed to want to help.

And now, here I was, nearly twenty-nine years old, just about to embark on a journey to another continent and put myself into a classroom. Was I crazy? No, I knew that I could read my Bible and I had my own teacher with me, the Holy Spirit.

The only way to definitely find out if I was truly dyslexic was to go and be tested. I booked an appointment with an educational psychologist. I knew that I would not be able to wear a mask any longer; I would have to reveal what I could and couldn't do. The day I was to go to the psychologist's came; my husband drove me to the appointment. I got out of the car, and I felt like that child all those years ago in the classroom, walking up to the house where I was to be tested. A woman invited me in, and we sat across a table from each other. I was asked lots of questions about myself; she was very kind and was doing her best to put me at ease. But I was feeling so nervous, on at least two occasions during the test I almost got up and wanted to run. The test was completed after two long, exhausting hours. I asked the psychologist was I dyslexic, to which she replied I most certainly was, but she would have to calculate my scores and send them to me. She said she was sad that at that modern school, they had not referred me as a child, as I could have been helped. She recommended a book to me called *Alpha to Omega*[18] which might help, and she said she would write in the report that I would need extra time in exams. I thanked her and left.

Happy to be out of there, on the way home, we stopped at a bookshop to get the book she had recommended. I felt the Holy Spirit say: 'I am the Alpha and Omega, the beginning and the end!'[19] I decided not to get the book, because I already had the Alpha and Omega. Not long after this, the report arrived in the post. I remember opening it and taking it to my bedroom where I literally sobbed for hours. At last, I knew I was not stupid but dyslexic. It was like something had been lifted off me. In summary the report had said that I had the intellectual ability, but that I had to concentrate on so much of the sheer mechanics of reading, writing and spelling that this prevented me from producing the quantity and quality of work appropriate for my intellect.

It was not long after this I had a phone call from my friend that I had been to Birmingham with, telling me that our host's husband had died. This was sad news, but I knew that the Lord had said to pray for his salvation, and that he would die physically.

---

18. Beve Hornsby, Frula Shear, Julie Pool, *Alpha to Omega* (Portsmouth, NH: Heinemann, 2006).

19. Revelation 21:6; 22:13.

My husband had decided that he would sell all the printing machinery, and another printer was going to buy the goodwill of the business and pay us a sum of money each month, which would go towards supporting ourselves in Africa.

The time was fast approaching for us to leave, and my thoughts had turned to where were we going to live in South Africa on our arrival. I had heard that overseas students live in temporary accommodation until they find some where permanent to live. I began to pray. I told the Lord that with four very young children, I wanted to know that we had a house to go to on arrival, and please could he send someone to help us? Within weeks, my prayer was answered.

My husband was going to a small meeting to be held in town. The speaker was from South Africa. There were about twenty men in all. The man that was speaking turned out to be from the Rhema Bible Church in Johannesburg!

Wow! God had sent someone all the way from South Africa to speak to twenty men in a tiny hall. Was he the person I had asked him to send to help us? After the meeting my husband asked the man how long he was staying. He said only for a few days, so my husband asked if he was free to come to lunch at our house the next day, to which he replied he was.

So, the next day he came to lunch; he was very excited to have met us and hear of our plans to go to the Bible school in South Africa. I told him about my prayer for accommodation, and how I had asked the Lord to please send someone to help.

He said, 'Well, here I am!' and he said he would help by finding us a house to rent. My husband then went on to say that he would send him some money to pay a deposit on a house and a month's rent upfront.

Not long after his return to South Africa, we were contacted. He had found us a house in a complex near the church and Bible school. He was also getting us furniture and a fridge. God had answered my prayer. So now we had a house to go to in Africa, we had sold the goodwill and machinery and the agent had a tenant for our house. All we had to do was say our goodbyes to friends and family. The group we had started had a big sending-off party. I wanted to visit all our favourite places so I could hold them in my heart. We went to the tiny harbour where we had spent many a happy hour with the children, playing in the stream that ran through the village. We then went to the beach to breathe in the salt air and watch the children play in the rockpools, this time paddling in their boots. Then we went to our place of shelter where the wind howled around, almost blowing us along to go faster; we huddled in our refuge, eating fish and chips. We walked on the South Downs, where we had walked so often before, visited the little village nestling at the foot of the hills, and took a walk up the lane for a final time, the gardens still looking beautiful even though the seasons were changing.

I bade a fond farewell to the little church I had entered some years before and met my Saviour when I had knocked at his door.

So now with all our farewells done and England locked in my heart, we locked up the house and drove to the airport with friends in convoy eager to see us off. Aboard the plane we breathed a great sigh of relief; we were on our way at last. All in God's timing, we had seen the Lord go before us, preparing the way.

We were all filled with so much excitement about what our next adventure would bring; we were flying from wintertime in England, and only the next morning we would be entering the summertime in South Africa. We'd be starting our studies in January 1991.

Chapter Five: On African Soil

We had flown through the night, arriving midday in South Africa, and were met by our friend who had got us the house. It was so lovely to be greeted by a familiar face and driven to our new home.

Our new home was a house in a complex of about twenty houses; the complex was surrounded by electric fencing and had bars at the windows and doors. This was strange to us. But the house was bright, full of light bouncing off the white walls, and we had some furniture piled up and the fridge filled with the basics. God had been so good to us; we had a home to go to and hadn't had to go into temporary accommodation. It was so central to where we needed to be. We thanked the Lord for his goodness to us and set about exploring the complex, meeting our new neighbours, who all seemed so friendly and welcoming, making us feel at home. Then we went to the cool, inviting waters of the swimming pool, where we all felt completely revived.

I remember the dusty red soil and the beautiful Jacaranda trees that lined the road leading to the complex. They were like beautifully dressed ballerinas all in purple, with great clusters of flowers hanging down. The birds were also bright in colour; one that stands out was the bright yellow masked weaver that had made their nests in trees by the pool, like little cocoons hanging from the branches. The bright shining sun set in the blue sky warmed us as we left the cool waters of the pool.

We walked back up to the house, meeting the maids as they finished their work. They were dressed in uniforms, wore berets, and some were in native dress – robes rich in reds, yellows, blues, browns, orange, green, all woven together to make a colourful pattern. The maids all seemed happy as they left the complex together, busy chatting.

Back at the house we set about making it our home when our friend arrived wanting to take us to see the church, Bible school and children's schools which we would be attending in a few weeks' time. We got into his minibus and drove for five minutes.

We arrived at the church complex. It was huge! The church could seat 5,000 people at one time, although the congregation itself was 20,000, and they would have three or four services on a Sunday. It was vast, it was like no other church I had ever seen.

Then we walked across the campus to the building that housed the Bible school. It was another modern building. As we entered we went into a large atrium full of light with plants in it. We saw the theatres where we would be having our lectures, and then in the same building was the children's school. We then went to see the little pre-school the younger two children would be attending and were met by the lady who ran it. On arriving at the pre-school, we were not sure if it was a nursery for the children or an animal sanctuary, as there were animals everywhere, much to our son's delight – guinea pigs, dogs, cats, hens, guinea fowl, even a small pony! We were shown the two classrooms the children would be in and were offered a cup of rooibos tea. They even picked a fresh lemon for us to have with our tea. After this we went to our friends' place for a barbeque and had a wonderful first evening in South Africa. Eventually all of us, totally exhausted, went home to bed. Our new adventure had begun.

It was the month leading up to Christmas 1990, summertime in South Africa. A lot of people had gone to the coast for the Christmas holidays. This was going to be a very different Christmas for us this year, no sitting by a log fire, no mince pies and no nativity play. But it was going to be a great adventure; Christmas in a different season. It was hot and we spent most of our time at the swimming pool enjoying our time together as a family and with new friends.

We needed to go to the shops to buy groceries and the children's Christmas presents. We were given a lift to the local shopping mall and on arriving there we could hear music being played: it was the famous song 'White Christmas'! This made me laugh. Much to the relief of the children, Father Christmas was here in South Africa too. After we had finished our shop, we were given a lift back to the complex by one of our neighbours. We realised that we needed to get a car soon as we could not rely on neighbours. Our friend offered us a car, but it was just too small with a family our size, so my husband and I started to pray for a car.

A few days after this prayer, at breakfast my husband shared that in the night, he had had a dream. In that dream, he saw a wooden instrument panel from a car, which he felt was a British one. I didn't think much about it, but he had always loved cars. After breakfast, my husband decided to visit some garages in the little car that our friend had lent us. He said to me that he didn't want to spend more than £1,000 on a car for us, and off he went. My husband had not been gone long, he was not very far from where we lived, when he saw a green Jaguar parked under a gum tree in a front garden. It was filthy and covered in gum from the tree; it also had a small dent in the front wing, and it looked a very sorry sight. My husband said he then heard the Lord say that this was his car, but it wasn't for sale. He had to go and speak to the owners. So, he pulled up outside the house and then knocked on the door.

A lady answered and my husband said, 'Sorry to bother you. I don't suppose you want to sell your car?' The lady was a bit surprised at his question and replied that she had not thought about selling it, but then told my husband that her son was a printer, who had just bought a printing machine. It had been expensive, the same type of machine we had just sold in England. She went on to say that her son needed to raise some money to help with the purchase of his machinery and maybe this was an answer. The lady then said, 'I tell you what, take it for a drive and see if you like it.' She went back inside and returned with the keys and some money and said, 'Put some fuel in it.' My husband promised he would return, once he had shown the car to me. It was so strange giving a stranger your car and money and letting them drive off!

My husband drove the car home. He began to clean a small section of the paintwork; right before our eyes he had uncovered this beautiful British Racing Green paintwork that shone. And inside the car was the wooden instrument panel that my husband had seen in his dream. He returned the car and bought it for a £1,000.

The car cleaned up beautifully and the wooden instrument panel was now highly polished. There was plenty of room for all of us and a huge boot for the baby's buggy and shopping. We thanked the Lord; we now had our own car to get to church and, in a few weeks, to get to Bible school and the children's schools.

In the complex where we were living there were a lot of young families and single parents that were working and would leave the maid to watch the children for a few hours, while doing their cleaning chores, until the parents returned. This meant that there were always a lot of children around that seemed to gravitate towards us as a family. One in particular was my next-door neighbour's little girl; she was seven years old, and she and her brother were alone at home during the holidays with just the maid, who was busy cleaning. The older brother would go and skateboard around the complex with his friends and the little girl would come to my house for the day. She ate with us and played with my children until her mother, a single parent, returned from work. We became good friends and when the children returned to school, I agreed to have her daughter after school. It was like having a fifth child; she fitted right into the family. Most days during that first holiday we had at least eight children with us each day.

We had made many new friends in the complex and even spent Christmas lunch with one family. We had settled into our new life in South Africa, and we had started to attend the church on Sunday, and the children their Sunday school classes. It was amazing being part of such a large church, but we were looking forward to starting Bible school, where we would be able to make closer friendships, as in such a huge church we would probably not meet the same people twice.

At last, the day we had been eagerly waiting for arrived. It was our first morning at Bible school and the first day for the children at their schools. We packed the children's lunches, and all piled into our newly acquired car, dropping the two smallest children off at the nursery. As we drove, the dusty red soil blew up over the car, and as we opened the door, the children were greeted by a white bulldog who proceeded to kiss my now giggling son. We took them into the nursery school to be greeted by a lady running around trying to catch a guinea pig that had escaped from its pen. Once caught, it was handed to my son while the pen was fixed. He then went off with the lady to meet his new friends in the classroom. Another lady came and took our daughter, now two years old, into her classroom where she was the youngest.

The two little ones now despatched, we drove to the Bible school and children's school building, and parked. We went up the stairs to the girls' school; they looked very smart in their new uniforms and were both very excited. Finally, it was our turn. We went down to the reception in the atrium. There were lots of students milling around, queuing to pick up piles of books that we were to read over the coming weeks. We were also handed our ID badges with our photos on, which we had had taken a few days before.

Once we had collected all our books we proceeded to the lecture theatre, armed with Bibles, books, pens and our files filled with blank paper. We went and found seats. There must have been at least 200 seats in all. I sat next to a woman who was part of a church plant in Iceland from the church in Brighton we had been attending. And on my other side was my husband.

We were known as 'first-year morning school', there was the 'second-year morning school' in the next-door theatre and we had a man in a sound box at the back of the room recording all the lectures. They also ran a night school if people worked in the day. We would have three lectures in the morning with a break for coffee and prayer meetings.

The first morning, the dean of the Bible school shared with us the story of how the church and Bible school had come into being. Pastor Ray McCauley and his wife had gone to Bible school in America at the Rhema Bible Training Center in Tulsa, and had returned to South Africa to start a church and Bible school. It was just the same as the church in Oklahoma. We were then introduced to the different lecturers, and they talked about the many topics they would be covering. There was clearly going to be lots of studying. The lecture theatre was filled with people from all cultures and countries. It was very exciting to be there at last, and scary at the same time. I was back in a classroom, not a place in the past I had enjoyed being. But I knew what it had cost us as a family to get there. And best of all, I knew the Lord had gone before us and had made a path in so many miraculous ways. I was so hungry for more of God, to know his ways, just to learn more from him. After all, the Holy Spirit was with me, he was my teacher and would teach me 'all things' (John 14:26), just as he had always done, but now I would daily be saturated in his Word, with the Bible being opened and him breathing life, colour, into the words.

Matthew 4:4 tells us: 'Man does not live on bread alone, but on every word that comes from the mouth of God.' It also says 'the letter kills, but the Spirit gives life' (2 Corinthians 3:6). I remember thinking to myself that I was not going to miss a word through the lectures we would be having; the words would be truly like honey to me. We were also told that each year, witches would come to the Bible school, posing as students. This was not surprising in Africa. Spiritually, the occult was rife, and some would consult witchdoctors. But I had been delivered of the fear of anything occult and was not worried by this at all.

We had been given a lot of practical information and had now met all of our lecturers. The first day was over and we went and collected the children, who had also enjoyed their first day and had made new friends. We drove the short distance home to the complex, where we were greeted by the little girl from next door and the children's many friends. We then headed down to the pool for hours of fun; the children jumped in and out of the pool, laughing. I didn't need much encouragement to join them as there was nothing I loved more than being in the cool, reviving water of the pool.

As Bible school went on, when the children were all in bed, I would sit down with the notes I had taken earlier that day in the lectures. I would always hurriedly try to get my notes down, not wanting to miss a point, which was still hard for me. I would have to interpret my illegible scroll and rewrite my notes. And as I rewrote them, so the Holy Spirit would breathe life into the words the truths I had learned. I loved those times, most of all sitting with my teacher, the Holy Spirit.

An illustration from Bible school, from one of our lectures, that really touched my heart, was on the Lord's provision. It was the story of a maid called Anna who had always worked for the same family since she was a young woman. She was now an old lady in her last weeks of life, living in a little shack in the village where she came from. She had worked for a lovely family, who had always treated her well. She used to clean, cook and do the washing, and she would often take care of the two children. She had watched them grow into adults and leave home. She went on to look after the now ageing couple; then the husband died and she spent time looking after his wife. She was a good companion right up until the end, when the wife became sick. On her deathbed she called her faithful friend Anna to her bedside, thanked her for all her years of loyalty to them as a family and for all her hard work. She then handed Anna a piece of paper, and not long after this she died. Anna was grieving for her loss and decided she would return to her village, and that was where she now lived in this tiny tumbledown shack. People in the village were always sad for her as she had sacrificed so much of her own life for this family, and now she was alone and very poor. She became sick, but she knew she would not be able to afford medicine. She did not want to make a fuss, so without medicine she too was now on her deathbed. Her friends came and spent her last days with her, and it was on one of those occasions that a friend noticed that up on the wall was a piece of paper that had been framed by cut-out pictures of flowers. She asked what it was and Anna replied it was the last thing the lady she had cared for had given her.

Her friend got up to see what was on the paper, and to her surprise it was the lady's will – she had made provision for Anna; she had left her a sum of money to buy a home and had provided for her, for the rest of her life.

You see, Anna could not read and had just framed it and put it up on the wall. She died without ever using what had been provided for her in the will.

The lecturer then went on to say that the Bible was Jesus' last will and testament and we needed to know what he had provided for us. This reminded me of when as a child my brothers and I had asked my wonderful grandfather, Dar, if there was a heaven and when he died could he send a letter to let us know? He had left us a letter; it was the big family Bible and in those pages was the answer to our question.

Over the last few months, we had seen so much of the Lord's provision in our lives, with the house, furniture, car and so much more. The children were also learning to trust God to provide for them. My six-year-old daughter was sharing with me that she missed her dolls' house, and Barbie dolls. We had only been able to bring a few toys with us. I suggested that maybe she should pray about it and tell Jesus that she was missing her Barbies back in England and please could he get her some replacements? So, when we sat down together the next evening, when it was her turn to pray, she as always thanked the Lord for a lovely day, and then she said, 'Please, Jesus, can I have a Barbie doll with long hair down to her ankles? Amen!' to which we all agreed.

This went on every night for at least five nights, when I said to my daughter, 'Do you think that Jesus wants to give you the Barbie doll?' – not forgetting to mention with the long hair down to her ankles.

She thought for a minute and said, 'Yes.'

I then said, 'Do you believe Jesus wants to give you a Barbie?'

Again came the answer, 'Yes.'

'Well,' I said. 'That's good – now all you need to do is thank him for them.'

So, the next night when she prayed, she said thank you to Jesus for a lovely day and thank you for her Barbie with the long hair down to its ankles; this went on for a further two evenings and then we saw the answer to her prayer.

When I dropped the children off at the nursery school the next morning, the lady who ran it came up to me with a big cardboard box. She said someone had come to the nursery who was going to Australia as a missionary and had wondered if she would like the toys for her school. She accepted the toys, but she said she felt the Lord saying that this box was meant for my children. I thanked her and put the box in the boot of the car to give to the children later.

After school with the children all now at home, I placed the box on the floor where they began to take out the toys excitedly, then my daughter, much to her delight, pulled out not one Barbie, but three dolls all with long hair down to their ankles, and lots of clothes for them! No one fought her for them as everyone knew that was her provision from the Lord, the answer to her prayer.

But it didn't stop there.

A few days later a good friend was coming to dinner and was bringing his new girlfriend to meet us. When they arrived, his girlfriend was clutching a little brown case, The children ran to greet them as our friend would always bring sweets. Then the girlfriend handed my seven-year-old daughter the little brown case saying, 'These were mine when I was little, and I thought you would like them.' My daughter opened the case and inside were another two Barbies and the case was filled with outfits for the dolls – with at least three wedding dresses, her favourite. When we laid all the outfits on her single bed it covered the whole bed from the pillow down to the bottom.

Not long after this, while I was just relaxing in the sitting room having finished rewriting my notes for the day, I felt the Lord say to me, 'You see that shelf over there?'

'Yes, it's just an old bookshelf,' I replied.

The Lord said, 'Yes but look again.'

I did and this time I could see not just an old bookshelf, but something that looked like a house for Barbies. So, over the next few weeks I set to work. I painted and wallpapered each compartment, making different rooms. I made little beds; I even made little patchwork quilts. I made a roof garden, with a basketball net made from an old orange net. I collected different bits and pieces to make furniture for her dolls' house. And the following Christmas, someone gave her a dolls' house kitchen!

My daughter had learned that she had a loving God who cared so much for her and every fine detail of her life; that he wanted to lavish his love on her, and that he hears our prayers and, in her case, had given her far beyond what she had asked for – he is an extravagant God.

The second story of God's provision was when my eldest daughter, now aged nine, came home from school one day, saying that she had wanted to go on a school trip to Gold Reef City – this was a theme park in an old gold mine. But we didn't have the money for it so I suggested to my daughter that she should ask the Lord if he could make a way for her to go.

At our prayer time before bed, she asked the Lord if she could go to Gold Reef City, and please could she have the money to go? Every morning she would check to see if an envelope had been pushed under the door. She did this as several times we had received gifts of money this way. But the school trip came and went and she was not been able to go.

The day that they had gone on the trip, she came home from school very disappointed and said, 'I don't understand why I couldn't go.' Distracted by her friends wanting her to come out to play, she then went outside. She had not been gone more than ten minutes when she ran back into the house, holding a party invitation, excitedly telling me it was next week and what was more, it was to Gold Reef City.

My daughter had learned that her loving God does hear our prayers and he does answer them, but not always in the way we think. It is up to him how he answers. The children were blessed with bikes, and we received a washing machine after we had prayed for one.

Another time we were blessed was when I forgot to give one of my daughters her lunch box before we left for school. I remembered it while I sat in the middle of a lecture. I still had one more lecture to go, and there was no way I could get lunch to her. 'Lord,' I prayed. 'Please provide lunch for my daughter.' I thanked him and carried on listening to the lecture, with a peace that only God can give.

After Bible school finished, we went to collect the girls. My daughter came running up to me, her face pink with excitement; she looked as if she was about to burst. Before I could apologise or even say a word, she blurted out, 'Mummy, Mummy, an angel bought me lunch.'

'What do you mean?' I asked.

She replied, 'When I realised that I hadn't got my lunch, I just went and sat in the canteen with my friends. As they ate, someone called my name. I turned round to see who it was, but I didn't recognise the man. He then asked me what I would like for lunch. I said I would like crisps and sweets. He said "No!", just like you do, Mummy! He told me I must have something savoury then I could have some sweets. After he bought my lunch, he just walked away. I saw him go upstairs and disappear.'

I was very curious and asked my friend who worked in the canteen who the man was that had bought my daughter's lunch. She knew everyone who that visited the canteen. She said she had never seen him before, he was a stranger. I went up the stairs and asked at the office there. No one had seen the man. So, whether my daughter's lunch was bought by an angel we will probably never know. But what we do know is that the Lord provided her lunch that day. God is faithful, always faithful. It was wonderful to see how the Lord provided for my daughter. The children were growing in their faith.

In Hebrews 11:1 we read: 'Now faith is being sure of what we hope for and certain of what we do not see.' We were seeing that we have a faithful God and if we believe him, he will do anything we ask for – if we do not doubt in our hearts but just believe.

But I do not believe that he would do things that are bad for us; like any loving father, he only wants the best for us. He has plans to prosper us, not to harm us, as we see in Jeremiah 29:11. I also know that according to 1 John 5:14-15 if we pray according to his will, it is an answered prayer; Jeremiah 1:12 says he watches over his word to see that it is fulfilled.

Chapter Six: The Baking Preachers

We had been living at the complex for six months now and we were asked if we would like to extend our tenancy for a further year, but we decided that we would not and we would move.

We loved our time at the complex, but we felt that we needed to be a little less accessible to all the children at the complex as we were needing a quieter time to study, and to spend time in prayer seeking God for what he wanted for us to do when we left Bible school. Also, we wanted to spend more time with our own children. We did continue to see the children from the complex, just not every day, and I continued to have my neighbour's little girl after school for a while longer.

It wasn't long before we found a house to rent just ten minutes away from where we were living. It was a bungalow in a large garden with a swimming pool and was in a lovely, tree-lined road. The garden was a bit barren and had a few plants. We had bars at the windows and at the door. We soon made it home and started to seek the Lord for his will for our lives. We were both so full of Bible school that we needed to release some of what the Lord had given us to others. Just like when I had come back from the Birmingham conference, it was the same need to put into practice all that we had learned.

We started to pray for the street in which we lived. We would walk down the road praying for each house. We would pray for God's kingdom to come. Mostly we would pray for the garden boys and maids who would all be sitting out on verges at the end of the day, chatting.

One day our nearly eight-year-old daughter was riding her bike with a friend up and down the road where we lived; the bike was a bit big for her and she wobbled and nearly fell off as she swerved to avoid some maids as they sat on the verge, chatting. One of the maids jumped up and started swearing at my daughter, who politely apologised for nearly hitting her with her bike. My daughter then said to the maid, 'You shouldn't swear!' The maid asked why not, and my daughter said, 'Because Jesus doesn't like it.' They talked for a bit longer about Jesus, and my daughter said, 'Would you like to come and meet my mother? She has just done some baking and I am sure she will give you a cake.'

So, the maid jumped up and said that she would like to come and meet me. My daughter arrived back at the house with the maid; she just ran into the house and asked if the maid could have a cake, and could I pray with her as she wanted to be a Christian? She then turned round with a cake in her hand, said goodbye to the maid and went back out to play.

The maid, Martha, told me the whole story of what had just happened; she said that the lady she worked for was a Christian, she had crosses over all her doors and went to church on Sundays, but she went on to say that she had never seen Jesus in this woman's life, but today she had seen Jesus in my little girl. I then prayed with her. My husband had been listening in the other room and came in. He began to cut off the bands from around her wrists that the witchdoctor had given her to ward off evil spirits. She began to sweat profusely and felt sick. But once they were cut off, she had peace, a kind of peace that only Jesus can give.[20] I told her that the Holy Spirit would reveal Jesus to her and that I would come and visit her in a few days' time. True to my word a couple of days passed and I went to visit her as promised.

Martha was sitting on the verge outside her employer's house, and I asked her how she was and what had been happening in her life, as I knew the Holy Spirit would have revealed himself to her. She took me by the hand and led me into her small room in the maids' quarters at the back of her employer's house. We sat down on her little bed, and she excitedly told me that the night after she saw me and I prayed for her,

---

20. John 14:27.

she received Christ into her heart. She had had a dream that night about one of her brothers, who she'd had a fight with years ago. She pointed at a scar on her face, and she explained that he had asked her for money as he wasn't working. She had refused to give him any and he had lashed out at her, and the scar was the result. She then went on to say that also in this dream she saw her best friend from years ago. She said they'd had a big fight and had fallen out, and asked me what all this meant? They were people that had hurt her.

I said, 'When you became a Christian, the Lord forgave you all your past sins, and he wants you to forgive them. The Holy Spirit will help you to do this.' I then said, 'Do you think you could go to your friend and ask her to forgive you and you can forgive her? Perhaps you could take her some sweets, something you know she likes. You should also visit your brother. I know it will be hard for you, but the Lord would not have given you that dream if he did not want to help you.' As I was telling her this, the words from the Lord's Prayer came into my mind – 'Forgive us our sins, for we also forgive everyone who sin against us' (Luke 11:4). She agreed and we prayed together.

The next time I saw her was the following week; she had been home for the weekend, and had gone to the house where her friend had worked years ago, armed with a bag of sweets, but she no longer worked there – she had moved away. I told her that it didn't matter because in her heart she had forgiven her, and she had gone to put her forgiveness into action. Martha then went on to say she had forgiven her brother. This was also an amazing event. The Lord had given her the strength and ability to forgive, just as he had forgiven her.

This was just the start. One after the other, maids and garden boys were coming to the house to receive salvation. Those that were saved came regularly for prayer and we decided that we should hold a weekly meeting in the house, where we would give a short Bible study and share what we had been learning in Bible school. We also preached the gospel and prayed for their needs, healing, family, and jobs for those that came. We would always have a wonderful time of worship where we would sing, clap and rejoice without any musical accompaniment. All the voices in the room would join together in harmony as we sang to the Lord – our African brothers and sisters did this so naturally. My husband would bake rock cakes and we were known as the baking preachers. On birthdays we would always bake a chocolate cake with candles, and on more than one occasion it would be the recipients first-ever birthday cake.

At these meetings we would see many answers to prayer, mostly people getting jobs. I remember the day that Martha's brother came to our house. I led him to the Lord in prayer, and then I prayed for him to find a job; if he would now go and actively look for work, God would most certainly give him favour. He had not worked for a few years and was naturally apprehensive, but he put his trust in God and went to find work. Within a few days, he had got a job. His sister declared the faithfulness of God at the next Bible study.

I soon realised that I had been given a special anointing to pray for jobs. I guess this was because it was the main need where we lived. People I had never met before would approach me at church or even in the street and ask me to pray for them to find jobs, and in the same day someone would come up and say, 'I am looking for a new maid.' It was truly amazing; people who had been unable to find work for months, after putting their trust in Jesus, were getting jobs, and those that had jobs were getting pay rises. My husband and I, both full of God, wanted to give out what we had received from God at Bible school. We started to ask him where we should go and to whom we should speak.

It was on one of those occasions that my husband felt led to go to a certain area not too far from where we lived. It was in the veldt. We drove to this area and on arriving we saw a group of boys, around twelve and thirteen years of age; they were all off their heads sniffing glue. Then we noticed a little boy standing alone; he could have not been much more than seven years old. The little boy was covered head to toe in dirt, his clothes were ripped and hung on him in tatters and the whites of his eyes were yellow. My maternal instinct was to get out of the car, scoop him up and take him home. We prayed about what we should do; we felt we should take him home, and then set about finding his own home, he was so young.

He was delighted to be in the car with our children. We drove the short journey home and gave him a bath, dressed him in clean clothes, and then he ate some food. I went out and came back with one of my friends, a maid from next door, to translate what he was saying. We asked him where he lived and how he came to be homeless. He told our translator that his name was Jacob, and he had lived with his grandparents, cousins, brothers and sisters in a little shack in a small community. He then explained that he had run away from home some time ago as he had to walk each day for miles to carry water home as there was no running water in their community; there was never much food either, and he hated carrying the water so far.

I tried to imagine my own son living in those circumstances and my heart ached. Jacob loved being with our children and would sit enthralled for hours watching my son's favourite video, which was in a language he didn't speak but was now fast learning. He would run around the house playing with the light switches, as he had always lived in a shack; taps with running water were all new to him.

We decided that while we could help Jacob get off the streets, the people he really needed were his family, so we went in search of the little shack. A few weeks later we found his family in a community a few miles away from where we had found him. We approached the small group of shacks with our interpreter, when an old lady holding a baby came out to greet us, pleased to see Jacob. They were so grateful that we had found him and had brought him home, but were convinced once we left, he would run away again. To persuade Jacob to stay, we said that if he was good during the week we would come and collect him every weekend to stay with us at our house. But in return he would have to go to school, and he would have to help his grandmother by fetching the water each day. We went and bought his uniform and paid his school fees in the hope he would stay with his family in the week. I am happy to say that this worked, Jacob went to school and helped his grandmother and came to stay with us at weekends. We would take him back after church on Sundays. We would bake rock cakes and preach a short message to a group of twenty in his community; this grew to forty in a short space of time.

My eldest daughter used to sit outside the shack in the dusty red soil, surrounded by children, where she took up the role of Sunday school teacher, drawing in the sandy soil. She usually shared whatever she had done in Sunday school, much to the delight of the children. It always amazed me, as so few of the children there spoke very little English, but all enjoyed it.

We would often go off the beaten track to various places, which some in the church considered dangerous, but we were there to share the Word of God and in return we found he offered us his protection. We would often go back to the same place with clothes, shoes and food, whatever the people needed.

As time went on, helping the people in these little communities, we met an amazing lady called Agnes. She was a lovely Christian lady who ran a soup kitchen feeding hundreds of people a day. She worked as part of the Rhema church, in a ministry called 'Hands of Compassion'. Agnes invited us to join her on her weekly visit to Soweto where she would hand out food to those in need. As we were white, we would have to hide in the back of the van with the children as we entered the township, Soweto in those times was a very dangerous place in parts, and many of the inhabitants hated white people, even those who came to help.

We would get out of the back of the van once in an area considered less dangerous than the rest, and help Agnes distribute food to the hungry, sharing the gospel with those who wanted to listen. We never felt scared in Soweto and neither did the children; we understood that when people are in God's will, we are also in his protection, something we found ourselves experiencing. This was an exciting season in God; we were going into all sorts of hidden areas in the township, or the small communities hidden in the veldt. We met all sorts of characters. I remember one such time when we landed in a small community. When we got out of the car, we were surrounded by a group of drunken men who had been distilling their own alcohol. There was one man that stood out among all the men because his hair was white; they called him Moses.

Realising this was not the best place to be with our children, we were planning how we would make our retreat. But we decided we were there, and we should share who we were and what we were doing there. We said that we wanted to tell them about Jesus, and that on a more practical level asked if we could bring them anything they needed, as we would return. They said that they needed shoes and that one of the men's wives was having a baby and they needed clothes for it. So, as we had promised, we returned the following week with the shoes and babies' clothes. They were all really grateful to receive their gifts, and the man they called Moses was very surprised that we had returned.

We were beginning to see that it's not enough to tell people about Jesus, but people needed to see his love in action; we needed to be his hands that reached out, touched and sometimes just gently wipe away the tears; the hand that would reach down and help pull someone up on their feet, or the feet that would walk into those derelict places; the eyes that could see the broken heart; the ears that could hear the unspoken word.

We loved those times out in the veldt in the rough bits of land where shacks huddled together forming little communities; we could see the smoke in the distance coming from their small fires as we walked towards the little corrugated-iron homes.

Life here seemed to be slow; the tasks for the day seemed to slowly evolve, from collecting the firewood, preparing the food, fetching the water and taking care of the children. Their lives were hard, and their days were full, but they always had a smile and would welcome a guest.

We spent many a happy Sunday afternoon in Jacob's community, where we would be invited into the dark room only lit by candles and the daylight that came in through the doorway. There was lots of laughter as the children played, and we would hand out our freshly baked rock cakes. There always seemed to be just enough. Then the baking preachers would share a short message, with the people intently listening to every word.

The seasons were changing again, and we now had been in South Africa for one year, but this year we were going away. We had just been offered a couple of weeks' holiday on the coast in a place my eldest daughter described as heaven, known to everyone else as Plettenburg Bay. We would have the use of a beautiful old country house in return for house sitting, while the owners went away. The house was very large for just the six of us, so we decided to ask a very good friend of ours from the nursery school to come and stay with us. She said she would love to come, and could she bring her youngest son, now seventeen, and his friend? We said that would be fine.

We were going to the house first, and our friend would be joining us for just a few days. The drive to the house was long, but very beautiful. We drove through the Garden Route, which was the most amazing coastline, and reached Plettenberg Bay, where we walked and played on the beach, which was miles and miles of golden sand; we almost had the beach to ourselves. This was a good place to spot whales and dolphins.

The scenery from here to the house was filled with tropical colour. The brilliant blues of the agapanthus, the vibrant reds of the red-hot pokers, the bright orange from the lion's tail plant, the spiky cactus warning us not to come near, and the strelitzia plant, better known as the bird of paradise. There were citrus trees – orange, lemon and grapefruit. There was even a plant that was likened to a tower of jewels, with its tower of purple flowers. There were brightly coloured birds and butterflies; it was almost as if an artist's paintbrush had been filled with colour and everything had been painted by hand in the most vibrant hues.

We arrived at the house, which was set in beautiful gardens. We were met a woman who gave us the key and we thanked her and went in; it was a welcoming sight. We had driven a long way and were tired so we just unpacked what was needed for the night and cooked a meal, and we all went to bed promising the children the next day we would explore. And so we did; the next day we explored our new surroundings. In the garden was a grapefruit tree that had the biggest grapefruits hanging onto bent-over branches, looking as if they were just about to fall. There was a gardener tending all the plants, busy at work. Then we went down to a paddock that was home to some horses. What a lovely place, we thought, to spend time, and there was so much more to explore in the local area.

We had been there a week and our friends would be arriving in a few days. Then we received a phone call from our friend, and she asked us if she could bring another woman and two children with her. We were not comfortable about our friend wanting to bring this woman. We knew a little bit of her life; she had some problems. I could not explain it, but whenever I was around her, I felt uncomfortable. After a lot of persuasion, we agreed she could come with her two children.

They arrived at the house during the early evening after what had not been an uneventful journey. We had supper already prepared for them. While our guests were sorting out their rooms, my friend told me what had happened in the car on the way there. She explained that while driving down the mountain to reach the house, the car had almost crashed and at that point the woman had said to my friend that they should go to be with the Lord. My friend shouted 'No!' and just avoided the accident in time. This made me feel even more uneasy. Later that evening when the children were all in bed, and the teenage boys were chatting in the conservatory, my husband and I and our two guests decided to pray together and worship the Lord. As we were doing this the woman spoke up and a man's voice came out of her saying, 'It had better be the right God.' She then spoke in her normal voice, and she got up and left us. My husband and I were shocked at what had just happened; our friend also looked shocked. I am not sure if we could really believe what had just taken place. And where had she gone?

She came back some time later. Apparently, while she'd been absent, she had approached a group of people who were playing drums. She told us they were Christian too, and they would love to come and worship with us. We said that we would hold a meeting in the barn on the day before they left for home. The next morning the man who worked in the garden and I had a conversation. I told him that we would be having a meeting the next day in the barn with some local Christians. He told me that he had a really bad drink problem and spent most of his time drunk, and that his wife was a member of the local spiritualist church. I then told him that Jesus could help him with his drink problem, and he said he wanted to know Jesus. So I led him in a prayer where he asked for forgiveness from his past life, and said he wanted Jesus to come and live in his heart.

I asked the Lord to set him free from the alcoholic spirit. I bound the spirit and loosed him in the name of Jesus – we have authority. As I did, he started to vomit up all this vile alcohol. When he had finished, he thanked me and left.

After this I went back into the house only to be greeted by a very oppressive atmosphere. The woman that my friend had brought to stay had started going around the house and was picking things up – for example, a walking stick, and she said it was vibrating and was from the witchdoctor. She then started to say she could see demons everywhere and in everything. Her behaviour was becoming increasingly erratic.

In the meeting in the barn, we met the people who had been playing drums. It wasn't very long after meeting them that we knew that they most certainly were not Christians wanting to worship Jesus, but who were they? Well, my husband said we should tell them about Jesus! So we did and at least half a dozen prayed for forgiveness and asked Jesus into their hearts. The next day, we decided to find a local church where the people could be followed up. It was a nice service, and we gave the pastor their details.

Just a few days later and we would be returning home. We felt a great sense of relief to be on our own again, now the others had left. Then in the afternoon a woman came knocking at the door. I opened it and saw it was a woman who had attended the meeting in the barn. She walked straight into the kitchen and when I asked how I could help her, she said that she was a friend of the man who had been set free from alcoholism and that she wanted it too! She wanted to be free from the demons that plagued her. I asked her to step outside, and just as I started to pray for her, she began to wretch and vomit, and I felt the Holy Spirit say to me, 'This is not me, it is counterfeit!'

I suddenly felt angry, a holy anger, and with authority I said, 'Stop this and put your false teeth back in!' She was shocked. I said, 'God will not be mocked.'[21] She turned and walked away.

---

21. Galatians 6:7.

The next day we would be making the long journey home to Johannesburg. We loaded the car and rallied the children and just as we were leaving, we noticed that someone had put a hornet's nest in our path. Without making a fuss and so as not to scare the children, we walked calmly straight past it and into the car.

On the way home, we both agreed that we had just had a brush with the occult and were glad to be leaving. When we got home, we heard about our friend's journey. They had been in a terrible car crash on the way home and the car was written off. She said that she had somehow lost control of the car, which had rolled over several times. Miraculously all the passengers, adults and children had got out of the car unharmed. Officials could not explain how such a violent accident had not caused any injuries. The Lord had most definitely protected them.

I asked my friend what had happened to make her lose control of the car. She said that the woman sitting next to her had said that her eyes had started to roll and turn white; next thing she knew the car was rolling over and over. She could not remember exactly what had happened. But she said she most certainly had not experienced anything like that before and there was no medical evidence to say she had a problem.

After a week of being back home, my husband decided to phone the pastor who had promised to follow up on the ones who had said they wanted to be Christians at the meeting. He told my husband that two of the people that had come to that meeting that night had died. Shocked, my husband asked why. The pastor said there was no explanation; neither were old or sick, they simply did not wake up in the morning. The pastor did not seem at all surprised. He said that they were all members of a spiritualist church.

We were both confused and shocked by what we had just heard. Goodness only knows what had just tried to come against us. It seemed the woman our friend had brought into our house had invited spiritualists to meet us, and had literally stirred up a hornet's nest. When we returned to England, this woman exposed herself to be an occultist in the middle of a church. At last, our friend had seen her for the person she really was, and no longer had anything to do with her on the advice of her pastor.

We will probably never know the extent of what came against us spiritually in Plettenberg Bay. But we did know that, as it says in Romans 8:31, 'If God is for us, who can be against us?'

In South Africa, it was not unusual to come up against the occult. I remember a Bible student from a Zulu tribe who came and sat next to me for several weeks. She was always very pleasant and wanted to be my friend. This student was wanting to get very close to me and I didn't really think anything about it; it got to the place where she wanted to move in with us. She was like my new shadow.

I was at a prayer meeting, and we were praying for different needs and requests from the Bible school. She turned to me and asked if I would pray for her as she said she was unwell. She got hold of my hand and placed it on her chest, and as my hand was there, underneath it I felt a pulsating and something literally moving. I pulled my hand away and the prayer meeting finished. Not sure of what I had just touched, I told my husband. He said we should see our friend who did some language interpretation for us as she might be able to explain what had just happened. I knew it wasn't of God.

After Bible school I went to the interpreter's house. She had met this woman at one of our Bible studies and had known that the student was wanting to move into our home with her young daughter. She was glad that I had come as she had wanted to tell me about this woman. She said, 'She is a *sangoma*,' and she told me that *sangomas* were witches, and I should not let her in our house. She was from a Zulu tribe and was basically from a witchdoctor. We did not let her into our house again. In fact, she was one of the people we had been warned about on our first day at Bible school. From that time on I think we became a lot more careful about the people we were allowing into our home, as our home was our sanctuary, our place to come at the end of a busy day to be with the children, the place our close friends could visit, and a place where we would pray.

I remember one late afternoon, the children were swimming in the pool with my husband, and I was watering a few very dry plants in the garden. As I looked down the garden at the family happily playing in the pool and at our little home, I remember feeling real contentment, and I thanked the Lord that the children were all so settled in school, and how I was enjoying Bible school and our visits on a Sunday to Jacob's community. It was then that I felt the Lord say that he wanted us to sell the house in England. This took me by surprise, and I was afraid. I had not wanted to sell our house, it was our home, our safety net; we could always return if needed.

I cried and said to the Lord, 'I am afraid. I don't want to sell our home!' This was a huge thing to do. I dried my eyes and went into the house. I asked my husband if the Lord had spoken to him, not wanting to tell him what I had thought the Lord had said to me. He replied 'No.' A few days later I asked him if the Lord had said anything to him and again, he replied, 'No.' The next day I decided to ask him again, for one last time. But this time my husband turned to me and said, 'The Lord has told me to sell the house in England.'

I looked at him and started to cry. 'That's what I felt the Lord had said to me a few days ago, but I thought it must have just been me!'

We agreed this was far too big a decision to make; we needed to talk it through with someone. We arranged to meet one of our lecturers from Bible school; he was originally from England. He shared with us a very powerful testimony of how he had asked his brother to sell his house while he and his family were in South Africa. And his brother sold the house, and then bought some shares on the stock market, thinking he would make some extra money for his brother, but it failed, and he lost everything. He then went on to say that the Lord had provided them with a house and everything they had lost.

After much prayer and deliberation, we decided that we would sell our home in England. We both thought that we would probably continue living in South Africa after Bible school. The next thing we had to do was get a valuation on the house and find out how much longer our tenants had got on their lease. This was the worst time that we could sell our house, as the country was in a very bad recession.

So, my husband made the phone call to the agent who was renting out our house, and when he came off the phone, I was shocked by what he told me. He said that we no longer had tenants and that we were in arrears on our mortgage to the sum of £2,000. We had ten days to pay it, or they were going to repossess our house. This was all really bizarre; why had they not told us, or sent letters telling us what they were going to do? If the Lord had not spoken to us about selling the house, we would, ten days later, have had it repossessed and not even known!

My husband flew back to England immediately, put all our furniture into storage and paid the money owed to the building society. He then put our house on the market and returned to South Africa.

While my husband was away, I had been collecting our mail from the PO box, instead of him doing it. One day after collecting the post I found there was an official letter addressed to my husband. I opened it. I was shocked to find that he had borrowed money from Barclaycard. When my husband returned, I told him that I had opened the post and had not known that he had been borrowing money from Barclaycard.

My husband explained that he did owe money, but the monthly income we received from the sale of our business would pay it off and we would get some money from the sale of our house, which after a day on the market had sold. With the country in recession, we were not going to get much money from the sale. Not long after, the money came through for the house sale, and all of the card overdraft payments made. We talked about our situation, and we decided that it was the rent of the house in South Africa that was our biggest outgoing. I said, 'Let's pray about it. Maybe the Lord has somewhere less expensive that we could rent.' So that is what we did, we began to pray for a new house to rent.

Not very long after this, our prayer was answered. We were told that there was an agency that had houses that had been repossessed by the bank. While the bank was waiting for a sale, people could live there in exchange for housesitting and showing prospective buyers around on open days; and they had to be responsible for the utility bills. We gave our notice on our current house and within a few days of registering with the agency we were offered our first place to housesit.

We arranged to view the property. It was in a beautiful road that was tree-lined and overlooked the veldt. As we drove down the road, we saw big, detached houses behind huge gates, one after another, and when we reached the house, we could not believe it. It was a beautiful, big, white detached property with a thatched roof, behind big wrought-iron gates. It had a lovely garden and a swimming pool in the shape of a shamrock. We then went round the house; it had an amazing front entrance with a huge spiral staircase going up to the first floor where we could look over the sitting room below. There were plenty of bedrooms for everyone, two reception rooms, a pool room and so much more. What an amazing place the Lord had provided for us! But we felt sad that someone had lost their home, and had it repossessed, the very thing that we had just narrowly avoided in the UK.

We agreed to look after the house until it was sold, and to be there on open days for viewings. We moved in. The house was completely empty apart for one room that we had not looked at during our viewing. It was a room that was filled with piles and piles of books, all piled up in neat stacks. My husband picked one up, and then another; all the books were Christian books. It must have been someone's lifetime collection. Later that day my husband called the agent and asked if we could have the books. He called the bank, who agreed and said we should leave what we didn't want in the garage. We went through the books and found ones we wanted to keep and the ones we knew our friends would appreciate. We decided there were so many books that just needed to get into the right hands, so we prayed where they should go. We even sold some, setting up a book stall at another Bible school that didn't have charismatic teaching, selling books about the Holy Spirit. There were also books that some of our lecturers wanted. This was such an amazing provision – a beautiful house, rent-free, and an income from the books to help with the bills.

I think the Lord was showing me again he sees the bigger picture; he knew that we were going to live in that house, he knew that the books were there, he knew who needed each one of them and he made sure they got them.

What an amazing God we have.

Chapter Seven: Provision

Living in our new house, it was too far for the garden boys and maids from our old home to come.

So, we would just pop in and see Martha and a few of the others. We did continue to go to Jacob's community on a Sunday after church and still had him to stay at weekends.

We were well into our second year at Bible school now and really enjoying it, we were still going off the beaten track wherever we felt led. We had also been to Zimbabwe with a group from the Bible school to a mission in Harare and we met the Shona people, who were very warm and welcoming. They told us that we needed to pray with them for rain, as there hadn't been any rain for three years and this had affected their crops, as they had been experiencing the worst drought ever.

The people were desperate and were glad that we had come to Harare, and they wanted to come to the mission, where some of the pastors from the Bible school preached. We prayed with the people and the leaders from the local churches. We had also taken practical aid. As Bible students, we were sent out to the streets for people who were always glad to have someone to pray with them, and our children prayed for other children. We had been able to stay with a friend from Bible school and their parents at their home, where they had taken great care of us all as a family.

It was a very long drive back to Johannesburg from Harare; my husband and I shared the driving and we saw a lot of wildlife, zebras being the children's favourite. There were great expanses of open space for miles and miles, parched land that was crying out for rain; we could almost hear the land groan in the wind, which blew the dust up over the car. The ground had been baked hard in the sun and had huge cracks;

it looked like pieces of a mosaic. I remember the acacia tree that stood alone, like a big umbrella that had frozen in time.

As we started to get nearer to home, at the roadsides we saw people selling beautiful, red watermelons. There were groups of men waiting for the white pick-up trucks that would pull into the lay-by, and in a mad scabble ten men or more would jump into the back of the truck, where they would be taken for a day's labour on a farm or building site. At last, we reached our lane, and we were home. We were greeted by our maid, Rose, who we had given a job, as part of our agreement with the house-sitting agency meant someone had to be there for people who may want to view the property. We all loved Rose, she was part of our family; she cleaned for us and did the washing, which was a great help to me when we were at Bible school, and she like to play with the children. She had a room at the back of our house. She had been part of the little group that had met in our home before we moved.

We were growing in faith at the Bible school and as the terms went by, we were learning so many new truths in God. Quiet evenings at the kitchen table with my teacher, the Holy Spirit, breathing life into the words on the page as I rewrote my notes, was still my favourite time. One night, after I had written up my notes, I felt the Holy Spirit say that my favourite lecturer would be returning to America. I was deeply saddened, and then the Lord said the lecturer was praying about this at the moment, praying for direction, and the Lord wanted me to tell him that he should go. I said to the Lord that I would.

At Bible school the next day we were in a lecture, and the lecturer was the person the Lord had asked me to speak to. He had been talking about people bringing words from the Lord, and how we should test the words, as when we receive a word it should confirm things the Lord has already told us. They would be bringing a confirmation to what we already knew. He went on to say, if someone told me to go somewhere, and the Lord hadn't told me, I would say 'go yourself'. Put off by what he had said, I was not bold enough to tell him what I had heard. So, at the next prayer meeting in the Bible school, I told the lady who led the prayer meetings what the Lord had said to me concerning the American lecturer, and she relayed the message to him. Not long after this he confirmed to the Bible school that he would be leaving and returning to America. And the lady that I had told was encouraged to go for further prophetic training after leaving Bible school. I had learned a hard lesson that we need to be bold and bring the word regardless of what others say!

We were now at the stage in Bible school where we had to preach a message to our class and the lecturer, who would be marking the message on content and delivery. The thought of this was terrifying me. I did not want to stand up in front of a class and preach. It was reminding me of the time I had been in front of the class as a child and had frozen. Nobody at Bible school knew that I was dyslexic, only my husband.

The week had finally arrived for me to stand in front of the class and preach. After much prayer, I was persuaded that I could do it. As I stood to speak, the Lord filled my mouth[22] and I preached. I spoke about the Holy Spirit, and how the Lord had revealed himself to me in the Baptist church and what the cross meant to me. I passed this part of the exam with flying colours.

So, we were in our final term and exams were looming. It was then that my husband became sick; he had started to get severe stomach pains. He could only liken it to the pain he had experienced some years before when he had collapsed and been rushed to hospital to have his appendix removed. So, confused by this, I started to pray for his healing, and as I did, I felt the Lord say, 'He will live and not die.' I thought that was a strange thing to say; my husband wasn't dying.

As the day went on, he started to deteriorate quickly. After an urgent visit to the doctor, we were assured that he simply had stomach flu and

22. Psalm 81:10.

were sent home. As we never heard of stomach flu, I decided to call one of our friends from the Bible school, as he was a doctor. Our friend just laughed and said that there *was* such a thing as stomach flu, and he told me to tell my husband that he would live and not die. This was the second time I had heard those words. I relayed the message to my husband, telling him that stomach flu did exist. However, he was not reassured by the message. I had never seen him so ill before and he was getting worse.

So we went back to the doctor, who sent us to a private hospital straight away. At the hospital my husband had a series of X-rays taken, as they thought there may be a blockage in his stomach. Sure enough they found something on the X-ray that they thought was old scar tissue from the removal of his appendix some years before. We decided that my husband would have to be moved from the private hospital to a general hospital in Johannesburg, as treatment at the private hospital would be too expensive. We were told that they would need to do a laparotomy, which is a surgical procedure involving cutting him open from the chest down to the groin, to see what was going on. It would leave a huge scar, which worried our best friend, who was a vet, as he said the wound would have to be kept very clean and this hospital was known for poor hygiene standards. He was afraid that my husband was at high risk of getting an infection, which in turn could kill him. He wondered whether keyhole surgery would be more appropriate as this would leave a small scar. I then approached the doctor, asking if they could do keyhole surgery, but they said a laparotomy was essential in case there was something else and with my husband's deteriorating state they needed to act fast.

Later that day, the operation took place while I waited outside with a very close friend. She was an amazing source of comfort to me and stayed with me until he came out of theatre. The surgeon came and saw me, and he told me to everyone's surprise they had found a Meckel's diverticulum, which is described as a second appendix growing in his abdomen. The surgeon said that this kind of condition was extremely rare, and he had invited several experts and student doctors to observe the operation.

The operation had gone well, and my husband was brought up to the ward. He was naturally disorientated as the aesthetic wore off. So, my friend and I waited until he was settled for the night before returning home to the children, as they had been left with the maid.

My friend tried to get me to eat something, but all I could think of was my poor husband lying in that dirty hospital ward, which was seriously understaffed. But I knew the children needed me to be strong and to reassure them that Daddy would be fine and home with us before we knew it.

The next day, after I returned to the hospital, I found my husband was on morphine for the pain he was in. I sat with him for most of the day and then went home to get clean sheets and pillowcases. I returned again that evening with our vet friend, who had medical experience – albeit with animals! He was very worried about my husband being in that hospital and the risk of infection. He told my husband that he needed to make sure that his antibiotics went into him, as his scar was very big and could get infected. My husband was afraid, as his drip had been disconnected, and he was worried that if it happened again there might not be anyone available to reconnect it for him. The time had come for us to leave, and my husband was pleading us not to leave him there alone in case the drip with antibiotics came out again; he thought he would die. We reassured him that he would be alright and that we would be back the next day.

That night he saw someone wearing a snake ring leaning over his bed and the next morning found the drip had been disconnected. So he refused to have any more morphine, as he realised that he needed to have his wits about him. But now he was in so much pain that he kept saying to me that he just wanted to be with the Lord, and he wanted to die, so the pain would go. I told him, 'Please don't say that!' We needed him as a family and assured him that God would bring him through this. I said, 'Have some morphine to help you and I will stay here as long as I can.' But he just refused.

As I sat there with him as he went in and out of consciousness, I remembered a lecture we had had at Bible school a few weeks before. The lecture was about situations in which people had the choice whether to live or die.

Later that morning I left the hospital and a friend met me and said that I should try to eat something, as I needed to stay strong for the family. I was crying out to God, 'Please don't let him die, don't let him into heaven!' We needed him and I loved him and could not imagine life without him. I was beside myself but my friend managed to calm me down. We pulled up at a restaurant and as we got out of the car, walking towards the building where we were to have lunch, I had a thought. I heard the unknown voice say to me, 'If he wants to die it's his choice, you can't stop him.' I knew how to answer the voice with the authority we have in Jesus, and always with the Word of God, so not out loud, but in my head, I answered the voice I did not recognise, 'You are a liar! I have a word from God, and he says, "He will live and not die."[23] And the word I have comes from a higher authority.' After that I had the peace that only Jesus can give, a peace beyond understanding, the sort of peace that when the Prince of Peace, Jesus,[24] walks into a room.

After this we decided that it would be better for my husband to return home, where I would nurse him full-time. He would be safer. I was shown how to carefully dress the wound daily and my husband was given antibiotics to be taken orally.

23. Psalm 118:17.

24. Philippians 4:7; Isaiah 9:6.

My husband was very weak for about five weeks, and he had lost a considerable amount of weight. Through continuous prayer, care and a lot of sleep, he recovered. As soon as he was strong enough, we resumed our Sunday Bible study at Jacob's community. Bible school was coming to an end and my husband had been through a tough time that was to determine the decisions he was to make concerning our future, whether to stay in Africa or not. My husband was talking a lot about going home to England as soon as we graduated from Bible school, rather than staying on, which we had previously thought we would do. I think the turning point for my husband was following his illness; it was a realisation of the dangers we faced while living in Africa. Although we knew the Lord's protection, there was a fine line between life and death there, and life was cheap. It was not unusual to see someone lying in the road after being shot; the children had seen this on more than one occasion, and we had to make a decision – was this the life we wanted our young children growing up in? I agreed with my husband. I didn't want my children thinking life was so cheap and could just be dispensed of so easily.

However, the thing I could not understand was, why we had to lose our house. I knew the Lord had said to sell the house; it would have had been repossessed and we would have lost it anyway. Or we would have had to have missed the second year at Bible school to save our house. Now we were thinking of going home but wouldn't have our house to go to.

I asked the Lord when praying about it on my own, should we go back to England? The Lord clearly spoke to me. 'Karen,' he said. 'You have a birthmark on your right ankle.'

'Yes, Lord,' I replied.

'And what shape is it?' Some years earlier a friend had remarked how the birthmark looked like the shape of England. God finally said, 'You are marked for England.' So, with that confirmed, how could I not want to go back to England, if that was where I was meant to be? I also felt the Lord say we would be used in the coming revival; now, that would be some adventure!

So, with us both in agreement, we decided we would return to England after Bible school. Once we had graduated, we began to sell our belongings and my husband booked our flight home.

The day of our graduation came, and we were dressed in our red gowns and mortar boards, and I remember thinking, 'Who would have ever believed that the little girl that could barely read all those years ago has just graduated from Bible school?' I was so grateful to all our wonderful lecturers. But mostly I was so thankful to my private tutor, the Holy Spirit, who had sat at the kitchen table with me in the evenings, breathing life into the words from black and white to colour. 1 Corinthians 1:27 tells us: 'But God chose the foolish things of the world to shame the wise; God chose the weak things of the world to shame the strong.' I was so glad that he had chosen me, and given me wisdom that only comes from him; we cannot boast in ourselves, but in him.[25]

With everything sold, including our car, and the suitcases packed, we said our goodbyes to friends. The house had a new sitter; it had never been sold, in fact, we had never, in all the months of living there, even had a viewing! It was with mixed feelings that we left. We had taken Africa into our hearts; it had been our home and we had made many friends, and there was sadness in leaving Jacob and his little community, which we had grown to love, as well as all the maids and garden boys, but we knew that if they wanted more of God, he would reveal himself to them by his precious Holy Spirit.

After a long flight home, we were met at the airport by our friend, who had recently returned from South Africa. She had borrowed a minibus so she could pick us up. We were all really excited to see her.

---

25. Ephesians 2:9.

It was early in the morning, dark and very cold, when we arrived. It was January; we all shivered as we were not wearing winter clothes, and had left the warmth of the summer behind. There was even snow on the ground, it was freezing. After getting off the motorway, I remember being driven down country lanes under a grey sky; I had forgotten how narrow the lanes were. It was very different to the blue African skies and the red dusty roads. I missed the warmth in the air and the colour already.

Our friend drove us to her mother's house where she was now living. We all got out of the minibus and ran to escape the chill in the air to the warmth off our friend's home. We were to stay here for a few days until we acclimatised to being back in England, and then go to my mother's, the farm, to stay for a week. We had no plans other than the next ten days.

Worried about our future and where we would live, but far too tired to even think, we all went to bed. When we got up we knew we needed to pray about our future. My husband said that he felt that it would be good to go somewhere different, as the church we had been part of no longer existed. So, we didn't have our church family. My dear friend Isabel had passed away. I heard that she had died while on her knees, working in her garden. This was a very appropriate way for her to die because her favourite scripture was John 12:24-25: 'I tell you the truth, unless a grain of wheat falls to the ground and dies, it remains only a single seed. But if it dies, it produces many seeds. The man who loves his life will lose it, while the man who hates his life in this world will keep it for eternal life.' I was really sad, as I never had the chance to say goodbye to her. I felt we were really alone, but I knew that the Lord had plans for us and he would show us where we should be.

Our friend said that we could use the minibus while we got ourselves sorted out. In South Africa, my husband had met a pastor of a big church in Wales and he thought it would a good idea to go and see it and maybe have a new life in Wales. This was all so different from the years before when the Lord had gone before us and made the way before going to South Africa. But one step at a time and we would find our home.

So, it was decided that we would drive to Wales before going to stay at my mother's. We left very early in the morning and drove the three-and-a-half-hour journey. When we arrived in Wales, my husband stopped the minibus to read his directions, and we looked out of the minibus windows at the vast, grey expanse of concrete in front of us. I turned to my husband and said, 'This isn't home.' He looked at me and suggested we went home, so without even going to see the church, he turned the bus round and drove us back to Sussex! We went to my parents' farm; my father was away. The children were so happy to see their nana, as was I, and the farm with all the animals.

Now back in Sussex, my husband went around the estate agents to find a place to rent, while I stayed on the farm with the children. They would feed the sheep, ducks and geese, and they would scratch the back of Porsche the pig, in fits of laughter, as he grunted, showing his appreciation. We played in the snow in our new winter clothes my mother had bought. The farm looked beautiful, all covered in white, like the icing on a Christmas cake. And there, outside the library window, stood the snowman all alone, while inside we sat by the fire eating hot crumpets for tea, surrounded by bookcases, sleeping dogs and the tabby cat curled up on the rug on the Chesterfield sofa. There was a smell of rosebuds and lavender from the pot pourri in the bowl on the round polished table. It was good to be home.

We had just finished tea when my husband came back; he told us he had found a lovely cottage not too far away for us to stay. We would all go and see it tomorrow, but now we had to help Nana move the sheep from the bottom field, up nearer the house. We all put on our new winter jackets, boots and woollen hats and headed down to the field to where the sheep were. My mother said, 'Just call them and they will follow.' But they didn't, they all started to run in different directions. This went on for half an hour, sheep and children running everywhere.

I said, 'Enough, Lord! Please help me! What is going on?' The Lord answered, 'My sheep know my voice and the voice of a stranger they will not follow.'[26] That was it, my father was their shepherd, and they knew his voice. But we were strangers, and they were running everywhere. The only way to get them to the top field was to stand in every corner off the field leaving the gate open and drive them up, which we did after a fashion, some even running into the field with the cows. At last, they were all back, even the stragglers, in through the gate into the field nearer the house. And made me think of how we are like the Lord's sheep, and we follow him, not a stranger.

The next day we went to the village where my husband had found the cottage just thirty-five minutes from my mother's house. The cottage had enough space for all of us. So, we went ahead and, with the help of a good friend, we paid a deposit and six months' rent in advance. We got our furniture out of storage and, with the help of my mother, made it home. The children had all their old toys back, things they had forgotten being new all over again.

We lived opposite a stately home in parkland; there was a lake, and we could see a folly from our bedroom window. We would walk in the grounds every day. There were deer in the park and the children loved it when they found antlers that were shed. It was a lovely place to play.

School was starting, so in a rush we put the children into the local schools. My eldest daughter was in the secondary school in the village where we lived, and the other two were in the school in the next village; the youngest went to a nursery.

My son was tested in South Africa and was diagnosed as dyslexic. I had all the paperwork with me from his test, but in England it was very

26. John 10:5.

hard to get the support needed to help him. I really wanted to make sure right from the start that he got the help I hadn't received. Help came through a dyslexic testing centre. There was a woman local to my son's school, who was training as a special needs teacher, and she wanted a pupil so that she could practise all that she was learning. So, my son became her pupil. She would go into the school, and he also went to her house after school once a week for lessons. Not many months later the baby of our family was able to start school and she joined her siblings in the very small village school, which had several years in one classroom. Not many months later, she too was struggling.

I began to pray about it one night when the children were all in bed and my husband was away. He was with an evangelist on a four-day mission. I wanted to tell the Lord how I was feeling about the children's education. I said, 'Lord, I feel really sad that I can't provide the education I wanted them to have.' I felt they were victims of our circumstances; they were living with the consequences of the decisions we had made concerning going to Africa and they had no choice.

Then the Lord answered me. 'Karen, if their earthly father can give good gifts, how much more will their heavenly Father give them?[27] Now go and choose their schools and I will provide.'

The desire I had expressed was from my heart; the Lord hears our heart. I had told him how I felt but he already knew, he wanted me to tell him. I was so excited and thanked the Lord and told him I would choose their schools if he would help me to find the right school for each child, all different if needed.

In the book of Hebrews 11:1 we read: 'Faith is the substance of things hoped for, the evidence of things not seen' (NKJV). Faith is also a gift from God.[28] I knew I had received the children's education from that

---

27. Matthew 7:11.

28. 1 Corinthians 12:9; Ephesians 2:8.

very moment, but it was to be tested. The very next day I collected the children from school, and took the children to the park. The children were all playing happily when my eleven-year-old daughter came running over to the bench where I was sitting. 'Mummy, Mummy guess what!'

'I don't know what,' I replied.

She then went on to tell me someone has written 'Jesus is Lord' in big letters in the concrete play tunnel she had just crawled through in the playground.

'Well, that's funny place to write it,' I said. 'No one can see it there.' We both laughed together, and she carried on playing. But I continued with the thought, 'If you are going to proclaim that Jesus is the Lord, you should put it where someone can see it.' Which reminded me of the scripture in Matthew 5:14-15: 'You are the light of the world. A city on a hill cannot be hidden. Neither do people light a lamp and put it under a bowl. Instead they put it on a stand, and it gives light to everyone in the house.'

Just then I heard someone say, 'Hello.' I turned round to see who it was, and it was my son's support teacher. She asked me how I was, and if I had had any further thoughts on the children's education, as she knew I was concerned. With great excitement I decided not to hide my light, and I told her that within the year all my children would be back in the right schools for their different needs, even if it was a private education. I just had to find the right schools and the Lord would provide. She looked at me a little surprised; she knew we were not able to pay the fees. She just smiled and went on her way. I thought of what I had just said and realised it was not long before the start of the new academic year. I thought I had better get on with my search for the right schools.

When my husband got home, I couldn't wait to tell him what the Lord had said to me concerning the children's education. He was really pleased by what I had told him, and we started to look for the children's schools together. We found that the local convent school was having an open day, and thought that that would be a good school for our youngest. We gave them a call and asked if they did bursaries, to which they replied they did not. Undeterred by this we asked if we could please come to their open day, and they replied we would be most welcome to attend and added our name to the list. We had a good friend staying with us who had been attending a conference in Brighton and I had already agreed to go with her, so my husband decided he would go to the open day. If he thought it was a good school, I would visit with my little daughter at a later date.

My husband arrived at the school and was shown round by a little African girl of no more than eleven years old; he said she was most polite and very enthusiastic about the school, where she was a border. One of the nuns asked my husband if he would share with her class, no longer than five minutes, about our ministry in South Africa, and my husband shared about Jacob and his little community. Just as my husband turned to leave, the sister who had asked him to share said, 'You remember you asked if we did bursaries and we said we couldn't? Well, we have prayed about it and we would be able to give you a small one. Please come back with your wife and daughter so we can show them around as soon as possible.' My husband thanked her and said he would be in touch.

The time came for us to return to the school, and we drove into the car park full of faith as well as being nervous! Before we went in, we talked about what we would say My husband said to me that she had said a 'small' bursary, it might only be £100 off the fees and we couldn't afford that. I reminded him that the Lord had said he would provide. 'What can we afford?' I enquired, and my husband told me £250 a term. 'OK, that's what we need to pay then,' I said. 'Agree with me in prayer that the fees will be £250 a term.'

'Amen,' he said. We got out of the car and went up the steps up to the huge front doors, the very steps I had been up as a child at a netball match tea.

Our little daughter looked really smart, and she wore a big smile across her face. The door opened and we were greeted by a sister who warmly invited us in, and then proceeded to take us around the school. We looked in on some of the classes taking place. When we reached the class our daughter would be in, we were welcomed by a lovely teacher and the whole class stood and said, 'Good afternoon, sister,' to which she replied, 'Good afternoon, girls, you may be seated,' and they all sat down. We watched the children interact with the teacher and they clearly loved her and hung on to her every word; the class had no more than ten children in it. After this we were taken to a little sitting room, where we were to wait for the headmistress to arrive. In she walked with a smile. She spoke to our daughter and asked us what we had thought of our visit to the school, to which we replied we had loved everything we had seen. She then turned to us and asked us if we would like our daughter to join the school in the new academic year.

A little embarrassed, my husband asked her about the small bursary that had been mentioned on his last visit. To which she replied, how much could we afford? Now my husband felt even more embarrassed and asked her how much was the bursary? He was putting the emphasis back on her! She repeated, how much could we afford? My husband again asked how much was the bursary? But this time she responded very differently; she bowed her head and after a minute she looked up and said, 'Well, I think £250 a term in fees, not in a bursary.' We were elated this was the exact figure we had agreed when we had arrived.

The headmistress said my daughter could start next term. I said that I could not wait that long as I was so happy. I asked her if they had any second-hand uniforms I could buy and could she start next week? Surprised, she turned to me and said of course she could, and we were led to the top of the school into a tiny room where we got all the uniform, including a blazer, for £5.

Every day that I drove my little daughter to school I would sing for the full forty-minute drive, praising God for his goodness and his faithfulness. I thought to myself, 'One down and three to go.' I remember telling my sons extra support teacher; she was delighted but couldn't hide the surprise and found herself saying, 'One down three to go!'

I replied, 'Yes, and in less than a year.'

We decided to look for a school for our eldest daughter, now thirteen years old. There were open days coming up ready for September's intake. We bought a newspaper and there was a public school advertising an open day, which was not too far away. We decided to go; it had previously been an all-boys school and they were just opening it up to girls. The facilities for girls were all brand new and the school had a high academic standard and a great ethos. We came away very impressed and were convinced this was the school for our daughter. We saw the headmaster who told us about government-assisted places; they only had three to give to girls that year. Our daughter was invited back to go through the selection process. She would have to take several exams and complete with more than thirty girls for a place. I always remember how smart she looked clutching her violin and her art portfolio as we dropped her off for the two-day selection process. She would have to board for two days.

Our daughter was a confident little girl, bright, outgoing and intelligent. She would be sent home from nursery school with a little tin filled with a selection of words cut out on pieces of paper that she had to read; she never liked doing homework and was regularly sent home with a noted pinned to her chest saying, 'Mummy, please make me do my homework'! I set her a challenge – in return for doing homework she could have a pair of roller skates, which she was desperate to own. This spurred her into action, and not once did she refuse to learn the words in her tin; by the age of four she was a fluent reader. Even today she can always be found snuggled in a corner reading a book; she claims her enjoyment comes from her love of words.

Three days following her return from the selection process at the school, we received a phone call saying our daughter had been offered an assisted place to cover her full tuition fees. I thanked them for the place they had offered our daughter and I explained with four children at different schools across Sussex it would be a challenge to get her into school on time each day. The headmaster then awarded my daughter full bursary for her boarding fees. In those days the fees amounted to £5,500 a term; what a marvellous provision God had been faithful to his word and had provided for our daughter. She was to remain at this school until the age of eighteen, when she left for university.

Two down, and two to go. We decided that our middle daughter should be next; again she was a beautiful, bright little girl, although more reserved than her elder sister. She always showed dedication and commitment in everything she did. She would have to work hard, but she always achieved her goal. In fact, she went to university after school gaining a law degree and went on to do a Masters. She was always so well behaved that when she returned from school, she would burst through the door in fits of giggles. Everything seemed to make her laugh; this was her way of letting off steam – we called it her crazy hour. She had large gaps in her maths due to the changes in her education and I set about finding her some extra maths lessons. I found a retired head teacher from a local school and invited her over to meet my daughter and to identify what her problem areas were. My husband was away, and I would not be able to commit to any lessons until he returned, as we would need to discuss whether we could afford them or not.

The day came and the teacher arrived to meet my daughter and assess her. They sat at the dining room table together going through her maths. I thanked her for coming and said I would be in touch. After the teacher had left, my daughter told me how much she liked her and was begging me, 'Please can I have lessons with her?' I explained that we needed to wait for Daddy to come home and we would see if we could afford the lessons.

Later that evening the phone rang and to my surprise it was the teacher; she had called to say that she had loved meeting my daughter and what a lovely polite little girl she was and so keen to learn! She went on to say she would love to teach her. I then asked how much the lessons would be. 'Well, that's why I called,' she replied. 'Your daughter is so keen to learn I want to give her the lessons for free.' I was really shocked and naturally I accepted the teacher's kind offer, and thanked her and God for another wonderful provision.

We had thought if the gaps in our daughter's arithmetic were filled, she could follow her elder sister when old enough to try for an assisted place, if they were still available. We did look at another school for our daughter, but we decided she was not ready to become a full-time border as she was not as independent as our elder daughter, and she wanted to be at home.

We decided that perhaps the best option would be to see if the school our youngest daughter was attending would take her for a few terms and then maybe she would get her standard up. So, my husband phoned the school and made an appointment to see the headmistress. Next day he was shown into the same sitting room he had been shown before and he explained the situation to the headmistress, who said that if our daughter was to attend this school, then this was where she would stay, pointing out that our daughter had made far too many changes in her education already. She was right, so it was agreed that our daughter would attend the school and take a scholarship exam purely to assess her standard of work, and she would then attend the school free of charge for the remainder of her education.

After my daughter had done the exam, with the help of a friend we bought her uniform, school shoes, filled her pencil case and she joined her sister at the school. After her first day, she told us how she had met her old friends who were at her school before we had gone to Africa, and how one of them had kept a rubber my daughter had given her before leaving. God was faithful and he had led us to the right school for our middle daughter. Three down and one to go.

I didn't want to make a mistake with my son's education. I needed God's best for him. I did not want him to suffer as a dyslexic as I had, so it needed to be the right choice. I did not want a school with a highly pressured academic environment. I wanted him to feel good about himself and be given the chance to shine and excel. I began to pray about it. 'Please Lord,' I prayed, 'I need your help to find the right school, as I need to make the right choice for him.' So, my long search began. I went to special needs schools, but he really wasn't that disadvantaged. And I visited state schools with special needs facilities, which meant travelling by taxi to access them and that was most certainly not what I wanted for him. I searched all over the county for the right school, until the day I knew my search was over. I found a small school in the hills of Surrey. The school was unique, because within the grounds of the main school was a separate building designed specifically for children with dyslexia. Its aim was to provide the children with specialist help and enable them to integrate slowly into the main school. The intense teaching techniques also aimed to help children pass their common entrance exams to public schools in their final year. We visited the school, and while looking around we saw several children wearing boiler suits to protect their uniforms while playing in the assault courses and tree houses in the woods. Our son commented on how great it looked, as he loved the outdoors. He was told that if he was a weekly boarder, he could keep his bike at school and go mountain biking in the woods.

When we met the headmistress, she was wearing a little fish badge, so I knew she must be a Christian. And the class my son would be in if he attended the school was called 'Omega', which means the end. I knew I had come to the end of my search; I had found the school for my son. The fees for a weekly boarder were around the same fees as my eldest daughter's school per term. I thanked the Lord I had found the school of my choice; now all I needed was the money to pay for it. So, my husband and I went back to the education department, who by this time had agreed that our son was to receive a statement of special educational needs. I knew I had found the right school, a school that could meet all his needs. We had many meetings with the educational department over the school we had chosen for our son, but we were always refused. However, I knew that the Lord had told me he would provide.

One day we received a phone call from a man from the educational department who wanted to meet with us at a nearby school. So, the day of the meeting arrived, and we drove to the school to meet with this man. We waited for him in a small office. After introducing himself he asked us about the school of our choice and why we wanted our son to attend it. After listening he said words I will never forget: 'I don't know why I am doing this, but we will pay for your son to go to the school of your choice.' We thanked him as we knew it was the right school for him, but we would need him to board as this school. He then agreed that our son should be a weekly boarder. Four down and none to go, and all back in the new academic year. We were overjoyed with the Lord's provision for our children; the Lord had said to choose the schools and he would provide, and he had done just that.

Shortly after my son had started, I phoned the school to speak to my son and a very polite, confident boy answered the phone. I said I would like to speak to my son, giving him my son's name and surname. Then the young boy at the end of the phone erupted into laughter and said, 'Mummy, it's me!' I could not believe my ears! Was this the same shy little boy who had left for school just a few weeks before? He, in such a short space of time, had become so confident and self-assured. He would never have answered a phone a few weeks before. From the very first day that my son went to that school, he had changed.

I have never felt so proud as a mother than on the day of his last prize-giving ceremony, as I sat with my daughters, watching him as he was handed prize after prize for his achievements in art, sport and his academic life. The girls said they were getting a bit embarrassed at one point as he barely left any prizes for the other children. My son had escaped the ghosts of my childhood and had grown into a confident, able and strong young man. He then went on to public school where he was awarded two scholarships for art and design, sports and received a wonderful letter of recommendation from the headmaster.

Praise God.

Chapter Eight: Sorrow

My husband and I had been asked by someone my husband had met during his time away with the evangelist he had been travelling with at the time if we would like to come and hold an evangelistic mission for them in Kenya. We prayed and felt it was right to accept their invitation. We would be away for around ten days in all.

I was beginning to feel worried that we were becoming dependent on the friend that had been kindly helping us with her financial support and said to my husband that we were needing to put our eyes very firmly back on the Lord as our provider. The Lord had used her greatly in helping us since coming home, in so many ways. She was a great friend, the best you could ever have; she had been there in Africa at the hospital when my husband was so sick, she had met us at the airport and taken such loving and thoughtful care of us, and even provided us with the minibus She would think about every detail of what we might need. It was not her provision that was wrong, it was more to do with us taking our eyes of the Lord and looking to her.

The Lord was challenging us to look to him and we decided that after our trip to Africa we would move to a small cottage where we could pay the rent unaided. We would put our trust wholly in God. We found a cottage just in the next village and secured it for our return.

We had flown to Nairobi where we were met by a contact of a big organisation, a large ministry in Africa, in fact the ministry of the German evangelist I had heard preach in the conference all those years before in Birmingham, Reinhard Bonnke. We were to stay a night in Nairobi and we would be driven to Lake Nakuru the next day, where we would stay with our hosts for the week of the mission.

Our first evening in Nairobi, we stayed at the house of a lovely couple and it was over a meal that we started to chat about our time in

South Africa at Bible school. My husband asked our hosts if they knew someone in the ministry, he was German, and he gave them his name; they thought for a minute and said they did. I said we had been at Bible school with him, and he was a great friend; he was a frequent visitor to our home. I remembered he also spent hours showing my husband how to fix the car, if ever he broke down when out in the bush in Africa. Well, one night he had come to our little Bible study with the maids and garden boys. It was during the time of ministry that I had a word with him. I remember saying that he had come to Bible school to find a wife, as in his mind that was the best place in ministry to do so. He was very specific about the kind of woman she should be. This was not unknown to me, but what I said next was revelation. I said to him that the Lord had asked him to go to Kenya to be part of the mission in the middle of nowhere, with not many people around, but he had not gone and instead went to Bible school in search of a wife he had not found. At this he had begun to cry; it was true, he said, for the very reasons I had said. And we prayed together, and he asked the Lord to forgive him in not going to join the mission.

Our host then went on to tell us that he was part of the ministry team in Kenya; he did all the sound engineering for the huge crusades, and he was now married, having met his wife – who had also been part of the team – and she was the specific wife he had prayed for. I think we all learned that night that God is able to do far beyond what we can ever dream or imagine.[29] He can bring someone the partner they've prayed for in the middle of nowhere, if that was where he told that person to be. God has the bigger picture. We shouldn't limit God to our own understanding, he is so much bigger than that. We need to see God outside of the parameters of what we know; he is the beginning and the end,[30] the creator of the universe.

---

29. Ephesians 3:20.

30. Revelation 21:6; 22:13.

It was good being back in Africa and a different part we hadn't seen before. It was much like South Africa, full of colour, beautiful, with breath-taking sunrises that would light up the sky in pink and orange, heralding a new day in a triumphant blaze of colour. It was as if nature itself was full of praise to the Creator who had called them into being. Then again at dusk, the brilliant orange sun lowered itself down behind the horizon and the majestic light filled the skies again in a pink glow that covered the scenery all around. Just the silhouettes of people could be seen: babies tied in cloth to the women's backs and the outline of little buildings in the distance.

We were taken into little communities often down roads full of potholes, where we would spend a morning or an afternoon with the people. Mostly my husband spoke to the men, and I would speak to the women, and then we would share together with the aid of our interpreter. We would teach on faith and how to believe God, putting trust in him, and letting him do the miracles. As we found so many times, they would have people coming with money for building a church. We were often taken to half-built projects, ready in the hope that the next donation would come in. All of that is fine, but we are the 'temple of the Holy Spirit' (1 Corinthians 6:19); when we ask Jesus into our hearts he comes and lives within us.[31] And we felt God was more interested in the people and changing lives, healing and making himself known, so people could build a relationship with him, than church buildings. This was different from what they expected. I think my husband may have been seen as just another Westerner who would be invited to speak and bring a donation, or go home to raise money for the project. They printed flyers with our picture on it and pinned them up with the ones that had gone before.

However, we did have some brilliant days sharing faith in the little communities, teaching them to put their faith into action, trusting God

31. John 14:17.

and allowing God to be God, not trying to give him a helping hand. I met and prayed with women that had lost babies and women with sick babies. One lady with a tiny baby asked me to pray, as she had two babies before that had died. As I laid my hand on the little life that was wrapped in a blanket, the baby smiled. We both knew that God had reached down and touched that little life. After the church service we would be invited to have lunch with the leaders, and it was always a wonderful time, sharing a meal with them that had been prepared with much care.

My husband and I also preached in the community's square, where I would always share before he preached. People would gather round to hear what was being said, and we shared the same message the whole time we were there – put your trust in a God that cares for you and is faithful!

Often before my husband preached, I would share the story of Anna the maid who had been provided for in a will, but she couldn't read, how the Bible was Jesus' last will and testament to us, and how they needed to listen to what the Bible said about provision. Then my husband would preach on what provision we have in the Bible, healing, forgiveness of sins and eternal life to those who believe in Jesus, just to name a few. The people would hang on every word, not wanting to miss out on the provision we have in the Bible; they did not want to be like Anna the maid!

The week was coming to an end and one of the little communities we had been to had taken up an offering for us and blessed us with a sum of money to take home. We were very humbled by this, it was so kind; they were not a wealthy people, but the Lord had used them to bless us as we had, in return, blessed them. The Lord was showing us that God could use the least likely vessel to bless us. I think a lot of what we had preached in Africa that week was also preaching to ourselves: we needed to put our eyes on the Lord and not people, and let God be God and watch him provide.

We had been promised by our hosts that we would be taken to Lake Nakuru National Park for our last day there. This was such a treat. We were driven around the park in the old car that we had had had all week; it was a bit worn out and had dents in most places. We just hoped it would hold together for our trip around the park. First, we went to the lake to be greeted by hundreds of pink flamingos. The sound as they all chatted together was like being in a huge arena filled with dancers that flapped their beautiful pink gowns and ruffled their black shawls as they lifted their wings. They were all walking on stilts as they elegantly made their way across the lake. There were so many of them that the lake had turned pink. Then we saw a rhino, which we thought was a huge rock until it moved. Our driver made a hasty retreat, and we drove on for a while, then we met a lion sitting under a tree, who lay there in the shade with his mate and cubs not too far away. He gave a majestic stare towards the car, and again our driver backed the car up and turned around! We saw elegant giraffes in the distance, munching on the trees. Then it was time to say goodbye to Africa once more, and we were driven back to Nairobi, where we caught our flight home.

Back on home soil once more, we moved to the little cottage that we had secured before leaving for Africa, now not wanting to look to our friend for financial support. We had seen how the Lord had just blessed us with a gift of money that was sufficient to be able to pay the deposit on the cottage and a month's rent.

Once we had settled into our tiny home, I remember standing in the kitchen and saying to the Lord, 'What do I do now?' I felt the Lord say to me, 'Whatever you put your hands to, it will prosper.'[32] What did he mean – what could I do? I looked in the cupboard that was almost empty except for flour, salt and oil. Just a few days before, I had been making

---

32. Deuteronomy 28:8.

dough animals with the children. 'That's it!' I thought. 'I will make dough animals, paint them and mount them on a wicker wreath and sell them.' So I set about making the animals. I painted and varnished each piece and glued them to wicker wreaths. I sold the first six and was able to buy more wreaths; this was not going to be enough money, but it was a start. Then my husband got a printing job part-time. The little craft business then started to take off and we sold the wreaths to garden centres, tearooms, hotels… wherever we took them, we sold them.

We were living in a cottage three bedrooms; the older two girls shared the largest room, we managed to squeeze our fourposter bed into the second bedroom, and the younger two now had bunk beds in the smallest room. The bathroom was downstairs, just off the kitchen, so every time we had a bath we had to make a mad dash in a towel upstairs to dry our hair before the cold set in. There was no central heating in the house; we only had a small open fire in the sitting room. My main memory of the house is that the sitting room could hardly accommodate the family, let alone friends.

Due to the size of the house, most of our belongings were stored in two old sheds outside, and over time, everything stored in them went rotten and damp and then had to be thrown out. The children would scrap the frost off the windows; even the hamster we thought had died and were going to bury had just gone into hibernation, it was so cold. It was miserable living there; we would take our life in our hands as we went out of the gate straight onto a country lane which was a cut through for busy morning traffic.

My husband had worked for two different printers, but having had his own business, was not happy working for someone else. He had just left another job, so it was decided that I would get full-time employment and my husband would concentrate on the ministry. He now felt that he should start a church. This was news to me. I had never felt the calling to be a pastor's wife. But I just wanted to see my husband happy and fulfilled in what he felt the Lord was calling him to do.

I got a job in a charity shop as an assistant manager, and after six months, the position of manager came up and I grabbed the opportunity to provide more for the family. My duties in the charity shop would be bookkeeping, writing up figures every night for different departments and cashing up. I was responsible for twenty volunteers; we always had a lot of fun. It was hard work but enjoyable. I also had to do report writing and even appraisals for my new assistant manager. I was surprised at what I was able to do as someone with pretty bad dyslexia. I would have to attend managers' meetings and go on training days. I also dressed the windows for which our shop won the regional prize.

My husband was now responsible for getting the girls to school and collecting them and collecting me after work. It was a long day. I would start work early and finish late, so he was responsible for picking up the shopping. He found a small hall he could hire in the nearby town, so we started to meet on Sunday mornings. We had about ten people to start, and on my day off I would evangelise for my husband, putting out flyers and talking to people. He was out a lot, even in the evenings, and I began to feel unloved and alone again. The school holidays were coming up and I knew it would be hard for the children to be entertained, although there were beautiful woodland walks to be had, so we could go foraging and on treasure hunts, as the children called it, looking for objects of interest – a rock or even some interesting leaves. Or we could take a trip down to the sea where they would gather shells, driftwood, old bits of glass that had been worn smooth by the tides coming in and out, and even dried seaweed which they would bring it home making beautiful big collages. There were lots of free days of fun out there to be had.

My husband was out visiting someone from the church one day when I felt the Lord say to me that he wanted me to write a book about how the Holy Spirit had revealed so much to me about Jesus, had healed me as a little girl, and had taken my Bible from black and white to colour. Excited by this, there was only one problem. I was dyslexic and would most definitely find it hard to write the story. It was later on that day that I had to go to the post office to get some paper, and as I was standing in the queue to pay, I noticed up on a shelf there were a few little toys for sale, and among them was a little red bus. On it was a billboard-like sign that read 'Holy News', and a picture of a quill pen. The number of the bus was 61, the year that I was born, and I knew then that the Lord was confirming to me his request to write; that's when I started to write this book.

The school holidays had arrived, and the children were all home, and I was at work. A lot of the time the children were left to their own devices to make their own entertainment, which usually meant a lot of mess to clear away. They were frustrated, as if they wanted to go to friends' houses to play, my husband would have to drop them off, and he often had to go out and wasn't available to take them. Our house was too small to have children over to play in the holidays. The children decided that they would clean cars in the village, and my husband would drop them off saying he would be back in an hour, but often might not come back for three. Then a couple of weeks into the school holidays my husband went out one evening and did not come back and I was really worried. I phoned around, and then I called the police. Next morning I had a phone call – it was my husband saying that he was sorry that he hadn't told me what he was doing, but he had gone to see a friend. I was really upset by what had just happened and said that we needed to talk. But he said it was all going to be alright. I was now starting to find it hard to leave the children while I worked, worrying that if he had left again the children would be alone.

This went on all through the summer holidays, until one day he went out in the evening just to go to the shops and didn't come back. He left a note this time saying he was sorry and would call. Next morning, he called to say he was alright, but I said things were not alright, and I said that we would need to talk to someone and have counselling. He then sent me a letter telling me all. He had been seeing people, and he had been unfaithful.

My whole world at that point fell apart and I was utterly broken. I felt like my heart was breaking. I literally collapsed into a heap and sobbed and sobbed. This was the final rejection for me. I must be unlovable. He did come home for a while, just to leave again. We went for counselling and after many months, we decided that our marriage was over.

I was now alone with our children and had to pick up my life and be strong for them. I was finding this really hard. The charity that I had worked for held my job open for a long time, still paying me. But I was unable to return to work, I was not strong enough, I was on antidepressants, and I went on to housing benefit to pay my rent. I found it impossible to get through a day without crying.

I was ashamed... we were Christians, and we were going to divorce. I knew that of course Christians do get divorced, but I had wanted so much for it to have worked out for us.

I believe that God used that very difficult season in our lives to bring into the open all that was hidden. He always uses that opportunity to bring healing and restoration or whatever is needed. But he has also given us free will.

At that time I had no church that I belonged to, and I really didn't want to talk to people about the hurt I was feeling. I shut myself away. A wonderful friend helped me with the children; she would stay all week and only leave me for the weekends. The children were really brave through these terrible first few months and we all decided that we wanted to move house, so I set about looking for a new home for us. We needed to leave this house behind us, and the sadness that had descended upon it like a dark cloud of sorrow. So, I arranged to be sent details of houses to rent in the villages around; we prayed as a family for a house that was still in the country, but not isolated, and one that would have enough bedrooms for everyone and had central heating and a bathroom upstairs and a nice garden. Also, neighbours with children, a big sitting room, and enough space for us all!

It was not long and our prayer was answered. I found a lovely house in a semi-rural area. I went to view it with the two youngest girls and my friend. On arriving at the house, I knew this was the place for us. The position was great, near to other houses but still set in open countryside. It was a good size and offered us the space we needed. It was double-glazed and had central heating. It even had a large brick conservatory that had the possibility of being a further bedroom. Not to mention the lovely rear garden. So, we went to the Citizens Advice centre, then the council and housing department. We came up with a solution that meant I could do part-time work and be offered support too, but it was to be later that I would get a part-time job.

After many forms were filled in, and lot of prayer, I received confirmation from the housing department saying that we would be given the housing allowance that covered the full rent on the house we had chosen. We would now have a lovely house that we could call home, and with the help of my friend, we packed up the house and my old landlord sent three men to move all our furniture and belongings free of charge. The men did all the heavy lifting. The oil tank had been filled up for us by my friend. And then we went with my friend and did a big groceries shop, and our cupboards were full. That night we all thanked the Lord for his wonderful provision and prayed that our life would be better there.

Over the coming weeks we started to explore our new surroundings; we had nice neighbours, there was a park near the house, lots of beautiful country walks and we were not far from the shops. It was pretty central to getting the children to school.

I still had a deep sadness in my heart and felt lonely when the children were all in bed. During the day, life was always very busy with my children who were at home needing lifts to friends' houses, dropping off at clubs and collecting from school in term time.

I was starting to feel really alone, and the Lord spoke to me about joining a local church. I had not felt ready to go back to church before, thinking people would want to know all about my life. I wasn't sure that I could talk about things without crying. And then I thought people would think that I was so stupid, not realising what had been going on in my marriage. But I knew I couldn't hide away forever; I was missing church, and being part of a church family. I missed the worship in the church and the preaching of the Word; in fact, I missed everything about church.

Even though I wasn't in church my relationship and love for the Lord never lessened. I just knew hiding away was not what God wanted for my life. The Bible tells us in Hebrews 10:25, 'Let us not give up meeting together, as some are in the habit of doing, but let us encourage one another – and all the more as you see the Day approaching.'

The Lord was also reminding me that I was not alone – he was with me, and he was not going anywhere!

Chapter Nine: Women of Light

Just outside the village where we were currently living was a charismatic community church that met at the local school. So, I decided that I would attend the church on Sunday.

The first morning at church it was wonderful to be back, to be part of the church body, the family. It felt like I had come home; people were very friendly and made us feel really welcome, and we were told a about a children's club that my youngest daughter went on to join.

I was still feeling very fragile and would often choose to sit at the back of the church, where during the worship times the Lord was just gently healing my life. The tears would run down my face, and I would feel his gentle presence around me. I felt the Comforter was present.

I began to know people and surrounded myself with a small group of friends that I knew I could trust, and who I began to open up to and share my life with. The church then went on to pay for me to go to a Christian counsellor, which I did for at least a year. She was a great support to me and helped me to recover my life. During that often-difficult year, my divorce went through and now I was single.

I felt a strong awareness that I now stood alone and was accountable for my own life; this had always been the case since the break-up, but I had felt shame, somehow guilty for not knowing about the hidden things in my marriage. I was now not taking antidepressants, and feeling much stronger, so I started to participate in church life. My son had finished his prep school and was a day boy at his secondary school and I had three children living at home, so life was very busy.

I spent a lot of my day getting them to school and back again all in opposite directions. And of course, school holidays were always busy. But we did have some lovely holidays together. One that stands out was when a friend paid for us to go to Cornwall, and we stayed in a lovely little cottage in Newlyn. It was a wonderful time as a family, and we made lots of happy memories there. We would visit little harbours, where hours on the beach were spent; we had visits to museums, lighthouses, a seal sanctuary and so much more.

That holiday was the turning point. Having walked on the beaches, feeling the salt air blowing through my hair, I had felt the presence of the Lord close to me, and now a lightness I hadn't felt for some time had come upon me, lifting the heaviness of the past. I felt refreshed. It can only be described as coming into a new season in God. It was like I had been walking in a dark valley, but never alone; I always knew his presence with me. But now we were coming up the hill and out into the open – an open space full of light, where everything seemed to be full of colour, and the grass seemed greener, having just been refreshed by the rain, the flowers lifting their heads towards the light. My life too was full of light.

The children were growing up fast and I was now able to work part-time. I started working for a Christian conference centre. They ran many residential weeks for church youth groups. It was not too far away from where I was living, and it was set in beautiful countryside. It was a small team in those days that ran it, and I was to join another lady on the housekeeping side of the centre. We had to clean rooms and change the beds before new groups came to stay, setting up the catering kitchens, cleaning the shower cubicles and what seemed like endless toilets. We would have regular prayer meetings, where we would pray for those coming to the conference centre that they would be blessed and enjoy their time there. I worked either mornings or afternoons; it was hard work, but I spent a lot of time talking to the Lord as I went about my job.

It was during this season in my life that the Lord was encouraging me to continue to write my book, and I would do this after work when all my duties of the day were done. It was being written by hand and I would spend hours writing and rewriting, then the church secretary started to type it up for me. It was taking a long time to get it down on paper due to my dyslexia, but I would always feel encouraged, remembering all that the Lord had done and was still doing – the story that was still ongoing and continuing to unfold.

I had been at the church for several years now, always sitting at the back; it suited me as it felt safe and secure. I wanted a quiet life, just an ordinary life, or so I thought.

This changed one night when I was in the sitting room by the open fire, and I had a conversation with the Lord. I felt the Lord was reminding me of the call on my life, and I felt a deep conviction. I recalled a conversation I had with the Lord when I had first started attending church again, a few years before. I had told the Lord I did not want the call on my life any more. I was afraid of the price I would have to pay; it had cost me everything and I didn't want any more loss or pain. I said that I had not wanted to give out any more; I didn't feel I could. All I wanted was to be in his presence. Now I was apologising; I was sorry for asking him not to use me and I didn't really enjoy this ordinary life.

I then went on to say to the Lord that I did really want the call on my life, being led by his Spirit, the adventures that I had enjoyed so much. And while I had been writing my book, I had found that I was encouraging myself in the Lord, reminding myself of all that he had done and actually longing for more. Then I prayed and asked the Lord to please give me a vision for what he wanted me to do. I knew that the Lord would answer my prayer, so that night I went to bed with a great sense of peace, and I was excited as I anticipated his next word.

I did not have to wait too long; it was just a few days later, when I was out for a walk on the Downs. This was a place where I found much pleasure. I could walk with the Lord, not usually meeting anyone high up on the top of the hills. It was a stunning place to be. The chalk paths I could walk for miles, coming across fields of grazing sheep, or fields with crops where bright red poppies grew alongside the wheat... The air felt fresh up there and there was always a beautiful sensation as it touched my face. Whether it was a cooling breeze in the summer or a gusty wind in the autumn, or a howling storm in the winter, whatever the season, I loved it.

It was a clear day, and I had a good view for miles around. I would always, when reaching the top of a hill, stand and admire the view. That day, as I was looking down, I felt the Lord speak to me and he asked, 'What do you see?'

I answered, 'I can see the villages below.'

And I felt the Lord say, 'To these dark villages, and many more like them, I want you to bring light.'

'But how?' I asked.

'I want you to start a women's breakfast, holding meetings in the village hall where you live. You will invite Christian women from the different churches, Methodist, evangelical, Catholic, Anglicans and many others. These people in turn will bring their non-Christian friends and I will draw people to the meetings. At these meetings you are to invite guest speakers with testimonies of how I have changed their lives and how they have come from darkness into light. You should share this with two people and meet for prayer, and when they have caught the vision, you are then to go to the elders of the church, and I will give you favour, and what I have said will come to pass.' The Lord also spoke to me about the book I was writing; he said, 'It isn't finished yet, it is still being written, and when it is finished, I will publish it, and you will see what I will do.'

On receiving this wonderful answer to my prayer for a vision, I thanked the Lord, but I also told the Lord I was afraid, and his answer to me was, 'Don't be afraid I am with you. Much will come against you, but I will not allow anything to upturn you.' With these words of reassurance, I felt ready and excited for my next adventure in God.

Just as the Lord had directed me, I found two people I would meet with regularly to pray, and they soon caught the vision.

After months of prayer and affirmation, I felt the Lord was telling me it was time to share the vision with the elders of the church, seeking their permission and their covering. I had felt the Lord had told me to say to them that I was not building their kingdom, but that I was wanting to further the kingdom of God in the villages, and that we would be inviting women across the churches. If, for example, someone from the Anglican church brought a friend and they found salvation, they would go to their friend's church or wherever they wanted to go. I believe there is a great blessing when the churches work together.

I went to the elders and shared the vision the Lord had given me. While they were happy to encourage me, they wanted to tell me that they only anticipated a dozen people would come, as this was currently the number in attendance at the already existing men's breakfast within the church. They had my best interests at heart; they did not want me to get my hopes up, for fear that I would be disappointed and worse, discouraged.

On hearing this I thought to myself, 'I know my God and how big he is and how faithful he is when he gives a vision. When he says book a hall and invite a speaker, he will not disappoint, he will fill the hall!' I thanked them for their views and concern and more importantly, their permission to go ahead. The next step was to share my vision with the church and put together a team, which I did, and then with the team I had a prayer meeting for the vision.

Now I had to find the speakers that I was to invite to speak for the coming breakfasts and book a hall.

It wasn't long before I had managed to secure some speakers for the coming months' breakfasts. With the speakers all booked, we now needed a hall to accommodate the meetings. 'Perhaps I should have booked the hall before inviting the speakers,' I thought. However, I had managed to secure some high-profile people, which people probably hadn't believed I would get! I knew I had been given favour with the speakers and I knew we would secure the hall for the dates I had wanted.

I had asked a friend involved that was on my team to go to a local village hall on my behalf. On my return from work, she had told me she had been unsuccessful in hiring the hall for our chosen date for the first breakfast; she said she had phoned around all other venues in the village and was unsuccessful in hiring anywhere. She went on to tell me she was discouraged and wondered if God was in it. I thanked her for trying to book a hall and went back to the Lord in prayer. I asked the Lord why we had not been able to secure a venue in the village for the upcoming dates we needed, to which he simply said. 'I told you I would use you where you live. Where do you live?' I replied, giving the name of the village where I lived. I remembered the blueprint he had given me. We had tried to book a hall in a village, the wrong village, and had not been successful. I phoned the hall in *my* village and, of course, all the dates we needed were available to us! I booked them successfully. I had learned a lesson – stick to the blueprint!

I had now got a hall and speakers booked. Sharing the vision with my church, I had shared the purpose of the meetings, the format and what I hoped the outcome would be. This was received well, and I soon had their backing, and a team of women to serve the people. We were known as 'Women of Light'. I was feeling encouraged, and now I needed to share the vision with other churches in different villages. The Lord had wanted Christians of different denominations to come together, taking off their labels and just being known as Christians.

I had prepared a statement outlining the vision. I also printed flyers, advertising the first meeting, and introducing the guest speaker and topic. I was excited to share it and in turn, people were catching the vision with enthusiasm. With only two weeks to go before our first meeting, I went out putting up flyers on lampposts, noticeboards, in shop windows and any available space that I felt the Lord led me to. The flyers had a contact number on them, so people could book their space to come to the breakfast. This was solely to give an indication of how many we could expect to be catering for.

On the day of the first meeting, and the days leading up to it, the phone had been ringing off the hook and even on the actual morning, people were still asking if there were any places left. With those and others that simply turned up on the day, we had a full hall. We had ninety-seven women, and the hall could seat 100!

With all the efforts of the team that morning, all doing their jobs, it came together surprisingly quickly; the tables were all beautifully laid, with a fresh flower arrangement on each table. Each person had carried out their tasks; someone had prepared big, cured meat platters with a selection of cheeses too, others put together fresh seasonal fruit platters with cut melon and strawberries, and we had bowls of yoghurt and muesli, as well as a large order of freshly baked croissants which were delivered from the local bakery. These were just a few of the wonderful things we had at our continental breakfast. I had several people on the door selling tickets and giving out name labels. The whole thing had been carefully orchestrated beforehand, with everyone knowing what they would be doing on the day. All the planning had come seamlessly together.

Before the meetings I gathered the team together and we would pray for the speakers, and the women who would be coming. There were prayer request forms on each table, so people could write down a request anonymously if they wished, and leave it for the team of Women of Light to pray about on their behalf. A couple of days after the breakfasts, we would come together for a prayer meeting to pray for the many requests; this was considered just as important as the breakfast itself. We as a team felt very humbled and found it a great privilege to go to God in prayer on the behalf of others – sometimes they didn't have a faith.

The very first breakfast, we could see that the car park was filling up fast and people were having to reverse down the road to park! We shrieked with excitement as we still had half an hour to go until we opened. Cars were parked everywhere, much to the intrigue of the local people. A long queue had formed from the car park to the door. Finally, we opened up and in came hordes of chattering, excited women, full of anticipation. We did not have allocated seats, which meant we had women from different villages and denominations sitting together, some Christians and others with no faith. They all chatted with ease at their tables, despite not knowing each other. As I stood there it became so clear to me that the Lord had placed the right people at each table with each other! This blessed me.

The guest speaker that morning was a great success and, in fact, the whole morning had been so good that women were booking places for the next meeting. Afterwards, I collected the prayer request forms and to my surprise there were sixty, all of which were about different things, many of a very serious nature. Whether big or small, they were personal to each person and of equal importance to God. Although we had only made a small charge for each woman, we had covered our costs for the upcoming meeting, hire of hall, speaker, food and any other expenses.

Women of Light went from strength to strength over the years. The meetings grew so much within the first year we outgrew the current hall. The bookings were coming in fast, the phone was ringing constantly, and it was becoming very clear that we had a lot more than 100 women coming to the next meeting – and we could only seat 100. Not wanting to turn anyone away, I prayed and asked the Lord what I should do. He said to me, 'There are two halls in this building.' The reason for this was that the old village hall needed updating and rather than pull it down they decided to build an entire new hall on the site, keeping the old part joined on behind the stage. But how would we manage this meeting being divided into two rooms with the stage in the middle?

The Lord had told me instead of laying up the tables in one hall, I was to lay tables in both halls. This was a great idea, but what about when the guest spoke? I was told that then I was to take down the front rows of tables and bring in chairs from the back hall so everyone could hear the speaker.

'That's a brilliant solution, Lord,' I said.

But we still had one crucial problem – although I knew the hall at the back had tables, we were without enough chairs. I knew how many chairs there were as I had counted them; I knew for a fact there were 105 chairs in total and we were already expecting 145 women to the next breakfast.

So, I said to the Lord, 'We don't have the chairs!' The Lord then responded with: 'You do have the chairs!' Rather taken aback at his response, I decided to ask him where they were. Then the Lord reminded me of the little shop that I was in the process of buying, which was to be my next venture. Of course, it was clear now; when I had viewed the premises I was buying, there had been 100 chairs left in the shop. They had come from the old village hall and had been stored there, and the vendor had asked if I would like them.

This was yet another amazing provision. What were the chances of having 100 chairs in the little premises I was buying? It was another example of God having the bigger picture; he already knew what I had needed before I asked him.

In that time, we had seen so many prayers answered and lives saved through coming together as a wider community and listening to others' great testimonies, which restored or gave faith to so many. The little village hall we met in were delighted to receive the gift of the chairs.

While sharing the vision, I was in a village the other side of the South Downs, and I had a God-ordained meeting. I had arranged to meet a really good friend – the one who had dropped in the little booklet

Journey into Life all those years ago. We were meeting at a pub for lunch. When I arrived at the pub, my friend was already there; he had got our drinks and was sitting at a table waiting for me. I had brought my flyers for the next women's breakfast and a vision statement with me. I had just started to show my friend when the door was flung open and a vicar walked in. He went over to the bar and was greeted by the publican as 'padre'.

There was lots of laughter. He ordered his lunch, and made his way towards a table near us. As he approached, my friend turned round and the vicar recognised him, calling my friend by his name and greeting him like a long-lost friend. They spoke for a few minutes and my friend introduced me to the vicar. He started to tell me that he was to be the new vicar in that parish; vicar, in fact, to three churches. As the previous vicar had not moved out yet, he was having lunch in the village, getting to know his parish.

He proceeded to tell me that he was coming into the village two days a week to work in the office. I then shared with him my vision for Women of Light and all about the meetings and what the Lord was doing in the villages. He was very excited about all that I had said, and he took my contact details. We both felt that we were meant to have met. A few days later he called me and asked if I would meet him again, to which I agreed, and this was the start of many meetings. Over the next few months, we would meet regularly to talk and pray together.

At one such meeting, he asked me if I would pray about coming to his church and working with him in the parish. At that time, I did not feel it was right for me, as there were some things that I had felt needed to be in place before I did that. For example, he was still not living in the village, and I thought that once he and his wife moved into the rectory, his presence would be there as the spiritual head in that parish. I continued to meet him and pray with him, and promised him if the Lord ever told me to go to his parish and help him, I would. In the meantime, I continued to distribute my flyers and share the vision in the villages and churches. I would always pray and ask the Lord to use the flyers, as so much of my life had been around words, print, and I myself had come to know the Lord through print. I had always valued print and its power to reach people. The Bible tells us that 'the letter kills, but the Spirit gives life' (2 Corinthians 3:6). When the Holy Spirit breathes into those words, they come alive, they have meaning, they bring life. The Holy Spirit turns words into colour and gives meaning – this is what he did for me.

So, every sheet and every poster were prayed over. I would always ask the Lord to use them to reach people to come to the meetings, and he did.

Before one of our guests came to speak, I received a phone call from a woman who wanted to book a place at the next breakfast. I asked her how she had heard about the meeting; she then went on to tell me that she had been out for a walk when a piece of coloured paper had blown towards her on the ground. She had picked it up. She said she wasn't a Christian, but the poster was saying how miracles still happen today, and she said she really wanted to come and hear the woman tell her story.

Another two ladies had seen a poster attached to a tree in a village; they were non-Christians as well, and came along. On another occasion I was in a meeting, and a small group of women were sharing the vision of Women of Light. I remember using an illustration and how even if we didn't invite our neighbours, the Lord was using the posters; the Holy Spirit was drawing them anyway.

On another occasion before a speaker came, a woman from one of the local villages was out looking for her dog, which had run off during her walk. She was very upset and a member of the Women of Light team offered to help her look for her dog, and gave her one of the flyers telling her about the meeting. They found the dog in a hedgerow, and she came to the breakfast. Prior to the breakfast, at the prayer meeting, our speaker told us she'd also had a prayer meeting in Sevenoaks, and a lady in had said to her that the women would be coming even out of the hedgerows!

The meetings were really growing, and I felt the Lord say we should now move to a bigger venue in the next village, which we did. This could accommodate up to 300 people. We had seen many answers to prayer, we had seen healings take place and often the prayer requests were answered in amazing ways. We used to have a time of testimony where women would share their answered prayer, but we had so many women coming forward that we had to stop those times, as there wasn't enough time to pray for people afterwards! However, we did get feedback, which was always positive.

Now that we had so many villagers coming to our meetings, the flyers were taken back by the village churches to give out. I did miss my times with the Lord putting up my posters where he led. But it was a great help. We now had people from more than twenty-five villages coming to our meetings and from at least thirty-five churches. I would also go to a village and hold prayer meetings with the churches leaving a lantern, a symbol of light, in their village. This was an exciting time in God.

Everything the Lord had said to me, I was seeing come to pass. He had said that people would come from far and wide, and they would know that God was with me. We were seeing the light of Christ going into these villages, through the Women of Light meetings. Women of all denominations, now without labels! People going from darkness to light! And while I was still having Women of Light meetings, my next adventure was just about to begin.

Chapter Ten: The Light House

One day, while working still at the Christian conference centre, I received a phone call from the vicar that I had been meeting with. He was phoning to say that there was always an open door at his church for me, reminding me that there was opportunity to work in his parish. He asked me if I would be interested in running the family service at the village hall once a month. He was just about to stop them and then relaunch under new leadership. Tempting as it was, I needed to work to pay my bills as the church would not be paying me, so again I turned him down and said I would pray.

I did pray about joining the vicar in his parish, and it was some months later that I at last felt it was right to join him. So, I saw the elders of the church that I had been attending for the last ten years. They said that they would give their blessing for me to go, and I was excited, as I knew God was calling me there. But also, I was sad to be leaving the church family that the Lord had given me. I knew that I would still be seeing many of them, as I was still having the Women of Light breakfasts and many of the team were from the church.

The vicar and his wife were now living in the parish, and it felt better knowing the spiritual head of the parish was there. So, after the service on the Sunday at my church, they prayed for me and gave me their blessing. I then decided to give up my job at the conference centre and moved to a small cottage with just my youngest daughter, as the older two children were away at university, and my son was in Australia on a gap year. I took up lots of casual jobs to earn the money I needed.

The church I was now going to was very different to what I had become used to. It was a traditional Anglican church in a historic building. It was far away from the worship in the church I had just left. (I believe neither way of worshipping is right or wrong, it's where we feel comfortable!) It was a new season in my life and in God. I knew I was not there to feel good and be blessed, I was there to be a blessing. I was full of expectancy, excited at this new chapter in my life, and I had made myself available to God to be a vehicle of blessing.

I had met a lady with a young son who had just moved to the area, she was from a more charismatic background and had completed a ministry course, and we became friends. Because she had a young son, she had decided to make herself available to the Sunday school, which was just being relaunched. We were both there at the invitation of the vicar, but she wasn't getting any children to go to her classes. I popped in to her class once and suggested she take the Sunday school as if there were lots of children! I remember she took a deep breath and gave a wonderful lesson on the tree that bears fruit – the gifts of the Spirit being the fruit, as we read in Galatians 5:22-23. She gave us a piece of paper and told us to draw a tree, which we did, and colour it in. I had drawn a tree and it looked like an oak tree. Her young son and I were then given coloured card which we were to cut into circles, then stick them on the tree with glue provided. When we had done that, on each one we wrote the words, 'love, joy, peace, patience, kindness, goodness, faithfulness, gentleness' and 'self-control'. We then went on to discuss them. She had also brought a lot of fruit, too much between three of us. She then said, 'Let's put them up on the wall.' We did, but her son was holding onto his very tightly and wanted to take it home. After church we went back to her house for lunch and had a lot of fun.

The vicar had not been in our church that Sunday as he was taking a service in one of the other churches in his parish. A few days later, I was at a regular Tuesday morning prayer meeting wondering why I was in that church. The vicar began to pray in an unknown language.[33] Then he stopped and turned to me and said, 'I don't know if this will help you

33. 1 Corinthians 12:10.

in any way, but while I was praying, I saw a picture in my mind it was a bit confusing.' He said, 'It was a beautiful oak tree, but then suddenly I saw orange fruit grow on it. Oak trees don't have orange fruit. Does this mean anything to you?'

'Yes,' I said. 'You have just described the tree that I drew in the Sunday school. Next time we are in church I will show you, it's on the wall where Sunday school takes place.' I laughed because I knew the Lord was showing me that I was where he wanted me to be. The following Sunday I got the picture from Sunday school and showed it to the vicar, and he said that was exactly what he had seen – the oak tree with orange fruit. We both laughed and I felt really encouraged. It was like the Lord was showing me that he knew everything that was going on.

I had said to the vicar before I had agreed to come to his church that I would pray for a vision for the church, which I had done. I had a picture of a blank loom, then all of a sudden, I saw all the coloured threads, gold, silver, reds, blue, brown, greens, yellow, black, grey, and many more. Now, as I looked again at the vision in my mind, there on the loom was the most amazing picture – it was Jesus, and his arms were held out wide, as if to embrace people. I just wanted to leap into his arms. All those threads had been woven together so precisely and had created this amazing image. 'How beautiful,' I remember thinking. I just wanted to stay there. But what did it mean? I believe it was Jesus himself, wanting to reach out to his people. I thought, 'How could anyone resist him?' He was so full of love, his eyes filled with compassion and all-knowing. There was an overwhelming sense of: 'I know just where you are, your every tear, your every breath.' The only way I can describe it is: 'I know you and I love and accept you.'

Then my attention was drawn to the threads, so many colours woven together. The image could not be created so perfectly without each piece of coloured thread. If it had just been two coloured threads it would just have been stripes; no, every colour was needed to make the perfect image. It was just like when I had seen a colour brochure printed; we would need the four colours to create the image – cyan, magenta, yellow and black. So, the tapestry needed all these colours to create the picture. The Lord showed me it was his people, the Church, the many different strands of his people woven together that would reflect his image. He was wanting to reach out through his people in the church to others with his love, and all the colours were needed.

In the Bible we are told that we are one body 'made up of many parts', likened to the human body, an arm, a foot and so on (1 Corinthians 12:12-31). The human body is a unit, though made up of many parts. So it is with Christ. If one part hurts, it affects the whole body. We needed each other to function properly. Similarly, each thread represented his people, all different. The vicar then asked if I would take the preaching slot the following Sunday and share about what I had felt the Lord had shown me concerning the church. I did, and the vicar's wife gave me her tapestry loom and coloured threads as means of illustration.

Not long after this I asked the Lord for a vision for the area, how we could reach out to the local community and bring light to the villages alongside the Women of Light ministry. I knew that when God gives a vision, the blueprint, all we must do is obey and the rest is easy – they are his plans, so we know they will succeed. We can all have good ideas, but we need the Lord's plan! Jeremiah 29:11 tells us, "'For I know the plans I have for you," declares the LORD, "plans to prosper you and not to harm you, plans to give you hope and a future." So, I set time aside just to pray for the vision.

Then the Lord gave me the vision for The Light House. It was to be a place where people could come and find friendship, both old and young alike. We would have a craft table and lots of toys. We would serve tea and homemade cakes. We would offer practical help to anyone in the village who needed it. And so we started The Light House, in the village hall.

We helped someone who had just come out of hospital after an operation; we planted a few bedding plants, as they couldn't bend down; we fixed a fence panel that had blown down in a storm. We loosened a stopcock for an elderly lady, so that in an emergency she would be able to turn it off. We also helped with filling out forms. These are some of the little practical jobs we did. And most importantly, we would just listen to anyone that needed to talk, and we'd offer prayer. This was just helping in a very small way, but being doers of the word, putting love into action, as we are told in James 1:22. This was not to build anyone's personal kingdom but to further the kingdom of God, like Women of Light, so we had volunteers from different churches.

One volunteer from the church in the village, who couldn't attend the meetings as she was working, baked all the homemade cakes for the tea we offered. She was an amazing cook; her job was in catering, and she was such a blessing to all who came and enjoyed her cakes. One village lady told me she had walked past the hall on a Friday three or four times before she had the courage to come in on her own. But one afternoon she came in and found out that we were warm and friendly! I talked with her, and she told me that her family circumstances had recently altered, and this was a very big adjustment for her to make. So, this was a big time of change in her life, and at The Light House she had found friendship and a group of people who were interested in her situation. She told me she didn't go to church, but she would always come to the Friday meeting at The Light House, and we became good friends. She then went on to help me with the setting up of the meetings, getting tables ready, and the toys laid out, and she helped with serving teas. She was a great asset to the group; we even had an Alpha course[34] run from her home. This was for the young mothers and older people who did not want to go out at night. The group was made up of people that had been coming to The Light House. We would watch a DVD while

---

34. https://alpha.org.uk/ (accessed 31 October 2022).

we had babies crawling around! We then discussed the video, and she would serve lunch. We would finish with a time of prayer, praying for people's situations and needs. And all those young mothers went on to give their lives to Jesus and became knitted into local churches. God was so faithful.

The Light House Fridays were becoming well attended, especially in the summer months, as we had outdoor toys laid out on the green at the side of the village hall. We even had a teddy bears' picnic where children brought their bears all dressed up to enter the best-dressed bear competition. One of the regular elderly gentleman visitors to The Light House turned up in his vintage car filled with balloons, and a friend dressed up in a large bear costume. Then the vicar judged the best bear. At Christmas he even dressed up as Father Christmas and gave out presents to all our regular children.

Around the same time as the teddy bears' picnic, I felt the Lord was laying on my heart to get my own premises, as I started to think how much more could be done if we were there every day and not just for a few hours on a Friday afternoon. I knew I had to begin the meetings somewhere, and the hall had been a good starting place. But the desire became an overwhelming need, so I said to the Lord, 'There is an empty shop in the village; perhaps that would be a good place?' And I began to pray for a shop.

I could hardly believe myself praying for a shop. I was working doing casual cleaning jobs, sometimes three different houses in a day. I was glad to get home to my little cottage! I didn't have to remind the Lord that I didn't have the money to buy premises, but I knew my God was a God of the impossible. In the village was an empty shop but it was not up for sale, so I set about trying to find out who owned it. I discovered that it was an elderly gentleman from another village who had put it up for sale, but withdrew it from the market when he found out that a developer was wanting to buy it. He would sell it to the right person. I gave him a call one evening and arranged to meet him at the premises.

The next day the elderly gentleman showed me around the shop; it was huge, and would need a lot of money to put it into a good state of repair. We could never have used it as it was. I thanked him for taking the time to come and meet me. After the visit I knew it was not the right place, but I was trusting God for the right premises.

I didn't have to wait too long; it was around three weeks later that the vicar was at a prayer meeting in the next village, part of his parish. It was a small prayer meeting of five people. At this meeting was one elderly lady called Milly. She was very distressed because the little building that used to house the village shop and post office was to be demolished. It had been empty now for three years and was falling into disrepair. It was on a bit of land that had been donated to the village and one of the trustees of the land was at the prayer meeting. Milly was praying about it. After the meeting, the vicar approached the trustee and told her that he might know someone that might be able to save the building. He said she should come and meet me. She did, the following Friday at the hall. She was a lovely lady and was very excited at my vision to bring light into the villages; she went on to be a regular visitor at the Women of Light breakfasts.

She told me that the building had a group of three trustees, and they were wanting to demolish the building and in turn dissolve the trust. I shared with them my vision and asked if I could view the premises. The following day I went to visit the little building in its very rundown state and I met a lady who had owned it some years before. Upon arrival she introduced herself and went ahead of me to disarm the alarm. We went in, and it was a dark, dirty, damp little shop. At one end was a counter with a cage on it where the post office had been. Layers of damp carpet covered the floor. There was a frieze on the wall, lots of shelves made from bits of wood, cages at the window, fluorescent tubes hanging from flexes, cables running one into another... There were also mousetraps and droppings on the floor. But as soon as I stood inside the shop, I knew that this was it. It was The Light House.

The only thing left in the shop was a case of Darjeeling tea and 100 chairs stacked up from the village hall as they had just bought new ones. I said to the lady showing me round, 'Look, there's a case of tea, it's a sign it's to be a tea shop!' It had reminded me again of the time I had previously been in the village – I had had a picture from the Lord of teacups and saucers. I could already see beyond the way it looked in its very sorry state. I could see it as a beautiful village stores and tearoom and in my mind's eye it was already beautiful. I remembered that that was how the Lord sees us; he sees us in our sorry state and then after salvation, he only sees us in a beautiful white robe of righteousness, his righteousness,[35] forgetting all that has gone before.

So, after my visit to the little shop, I went to meet the trustees. They were not a church group although one was on the parish council. I shared with them what I proposed to do there, and it was agreed; they would stand down as trustees and I would appoint my own, which I did with the help of a Christian solicitor. This was independent of the church, and it took around seven months to sort out. Then finally the day came when I bought the shop, the papers were signed, I paid £1 for the shop and was handed the keys. The £1 was then handed back to me as a donation to the work of The Light House.

With the help of family and friends I began the hard task of clearing the shop of all the debris. Often, I would work there alone in the freezing cold and leave after dark. I was still cleaning houses during the day. My son, now back from Australia, came and worked with me and without him, The Light House would not be what it is today. With the vision of how the Lord wanted it to be, and my son's God-given ability to work

---

35. 1 Corinthians 1:30.

with wood, we set about bringing The Light House village stores and tearoom into being.

I knew where the new windows would be and where the second door was to be put in, the colour, everything, just like when the tabernacle was built in the book of Exodus,[36] every detail. But I didn't have the money to complete such a project. No, but I knew with the vision comes provision!

The first thing after the shop had been cleared would be to rewire it, and replace all the fluorescent tubes. Then my son would fit a new door and put in two new windows to fill it with light and a view of the wonderful horse chestnut tree just outside, and the green that the shop stood in. All the plasterboard on the walls and ceiling was damp and would have to be pulled down and replaced.

I opened a Light House bank account and paid in the money that I had, along with a small amount that friends had given me. The cheques would have to be signed by myself and one or other of my trustees. I got a local electrician to give me a quote, along with two others. Works were agreed with the local electrician, who over the next month would come in sometimes in the day, or work in the evenings, as he lived just over the road. My son also came and worked when he had the time. He put up all new plasterboard which had been donated by the local builders' merchant in the village, lots of odd sheets, but it didn't matter as it would be plastered over. My son put in two new windows and a new door and made beautiful shutters for the windows. The outside of the building was now painted white, and we painted the new shutters a pale grey.

It was on one occasion that my son was working on the outside of the building, putting cedar shingle tiles on the roof of the veranda that wound round the outside of the building and I stood back to admire it and I said to my son we need something over the door. No sooner than

---

36. See Exodus 26.

the words had come out of my mouth, a car pulled up. It was a friend. He jumped out to have a look at the shop and said he had something in the car for my garden and should he drop it off for me?

'What is it?' I enquired. He told me to come and have a look, and in his car was the most enormous triangle-shaped dovecote. 'That's it!' I cried. 'It's perfect to go above my door here.' My son put it up for me and the base was the perfect fit, the same width as the wide doorframe. It looked perfect; it was an old antique dovecote and it was already painted grey.

The electrics were nearly finished in the shop, the wires were hanging down through the holes in the ceiling where the spotlights would go, and the metal boxes were in place ready for the power points.

The money was fast running out and the shop was ready to be plastered. So, I phoned around for some quotes. The first quote was for £800 to do the whole shop, walls and ceiling, but I felt I should get another quote. The next quote was £500. I thought that was really good, but the money didn't come in. I prayed and asked the Lord why the money had not come in, as that was a really good price. But there was just silence.

I talked with some of the young mothers from The Light House about fundraising and we did a fancy dress one Friday afternoon. One of the women suggested a raffle. I agreed and set about getting some prizes. The local garden centre donated a huge teacup and saucer filled with plants. The pub gave us dinner for two, a restaurant gave us wine. We were also given sweets and soft toys; we were given favour wherever we went. Once we got all the prizes, I gave a book of raffle tickets to the vicar and one to my friends who hosted the Alpha course; I had one for myself and another I gave to one of the young mothers. We set about selling them, and it was a week later at the lunchtime Alpha meeting that I announced to the group that I would have to leave early because I was meeting a plasterer at the shop to give me a quote. So, I then said to them, 'Agree with me in prayer that whatever amount we have raised so far will cover the cost of the quote for the plastering.' One of them asked how they agreed with me in prayer. I said, 'I will pray and ask the Lord and at the end you say "Amen", that means so be it!' So, I prayed, and they all said, 'Amen!'

I set off in the car the five-minute journey to the shop. When I arrived the plasterer was already standing outside with a young man who turned out to be his apprentice. The plasterer looked at the job and said that they could come back the following week and spend a long day there and between them get the job done at the cost of £380. 'Wow!' I said. 'That's fantastic!' We agreed the price and he said that he would come early in the morning next week.

I thanked him and drove back to the Alpha meeting, and everyone was still there. Very excited at the quote I had been given, I told the small group and said, 'Let's put all the money we've got so far with the vicar's, and count it.' So, I counted out the money and it was exactly £380. Someone pointed out that this was weird, and we counted it again and got the same figure. 'That's amazing!' someone shouted. And I said, 'That's my God, that's my God!' Everyone cheered with excitement. What a brilliant way to finish an Alpha meeting.

The following week I was to have a minor operation. It was day surgery and a few days after that the plasterers would come. The morning I was to have the surgery I had a phone call from my good friend with the little son from the church and she said that she felt she needed to tell me that I was in the Lord's hands. I thanked her and said I would see her after the operation. No sooner had she given me the message than the vicar phoned and said the same words, that I was in the Lord's hands. I thanked him and said I would see him in a few days. My two daughters took me to the hospital, where they would wait for me to have surgery and then take me home.

I was the first to go to theatre. I remember the anaesthetic, then waking up with fluid being pumped into me and an oxygen mask on my face. I was on a trolley and I was about to be rushed by ambulance to a nearby hospital. I had haemorrhaged and they had found it hard to stop the bleeding. I had become tachycardic. My poor daughters had waited for hours for news, only to be told I wasn't out of the woods yet. Finally, my eldest daughter demanded, 'I want to see my mother now!' and they were allowed to see me being put into the ambulance.

While in the ambulance the words came back to me, 'You're in the Lord's hands' and I knew that I was. He had brought me through the crisis, and I was safe, I was in his hands.

I had to stay in hospital for three days. On the day that I left, my friend came to the house to take me to the shop to pay the plasterers; they had done a really good job and the shop was starting to look great. She then took me home – my little cottage was filled with flowers. It took me time to really recover from the surgery as I felt very tired, but two weeks on, I was back to work and The Light House project.

On my way to my first cleaning job, I called in at my friends' house they were pleased to see me fit and well again. I told them how wonderful the shop was looking and that I needed to do the flooring next. I wanted laminated flooring, but my friends said that would be too expensive. So, I tried to rethink what I could use, but in my blueprint from God, it was laminate flooring!

I then went to my first job; it was an elderly lady who was living in her daughter's house. She had her own large sitting room and when I had last seen her, they were getting the decorators in to paint. She was really pleased to see me back at work. I asked her how it was going, and she said it was all painted; she was just waiting for the carpet fitters to come and take up the laminate flooring and lay carpet for her. 'Laminate?' I said. 'Did you say laminate? Can you reuse it once it's taken up?' She said she wasn't sure. I then said, 'Could I have it for The Light House shop?'

She said I could; she was having to pay the fitters to take it away. After I finished cleaning, she promised to phone me once the fitters had taken the flooring up, and in return, I said that my son would come to collect it. The flooring was perfect; it was a light-colour wood, just as I had envisaged. That was an amazing provision. What was next? I had just bought an ex-display sink, a large butler sink, and I now needed worktops and a counter.

My son was now away working and staying in London. He was fitting a kitchen and staying at the client's house. One evening, he was just returning to the house where he was staying, and he saw some beautiful old oak-panelled shutters in a skip right outside a Georgian property. He looked at them, and then looked again. He thought that they would be brilliant with some work, and if cut down, they would make a front for the counter. He knocked on the door of the house and asked if he could have them, and the reply was to help himself. My son was very excited and phoned to tell me about them, but he wasn't sure how he would get them home from London, as he was in his girlfriend's small car and not in his truck. 'Somehow,' he said, 'I will make a way.' The next day he tied them to the roof of the car and made the journey home.

Then my really good friend, who was also trustee of the land, took them to her husband's joinery business, also in the village, and they came back cut down and polished; they had made a set of large drawers to go under the counter. It was a real feature; the oak counter was beautiful. I thanked her for the work the joiners had done on them and praised God for another amazing provision.

Now I would need some worktops. I had felt the Lord telling me to write a letter to a kitchen supplier, to ask them if they had any ex-display counters. They were a high-quality local kitchen company. I had written the letter but had not got around to sending it. In the meantime, I had

had other suggestions from people – one was to put an advert in the parish magazine. Another said that they were having work done at their house and the man doing it had a contact that took out old kitchens. All these suggestions were followed up, taking up a lot of time and they were all dead ends. I prayed and asked the Lord why the kitchen hadn't come in, as my son was coming into the shop in less than a week to fit it?

The Lord said, 'Have you done what I asked you to do?' I thought for a minute, and I remembered the letter the Lord had asked me to write some six weeks before and I hadn't posted. I told the Lord I was sorry that I hadn't sent it and instead I would go and deliver the letter in person, which I did. It was a huge company on an industrial estate. It made bespoke kitchens. I spoke to the receptionist who said she would pass the letter on to the right person. I gave her my phone number and she said she would call if anything came up. I thanked her and walked back to my car thinking, 'Well, that's all I can do.' At least I had now done what I should have done weeks ago! The very next day I had a call from the kitchen company saying, they had a worktop and a cupboard for our sink, could I come and collect it? Excitedly I told them that I would arrange it. I phoned my friend who had a jeep and she said she and her husband would collect it the next day.

When she and her husband arrived at the kitchen company, they said they had come to collect the donated goods for The Light House, and were directed to a loading bay. To my friend's delight, there was a very expensive kitchen unit and worktop in exactly the right grey that we had painted the veranda and shutters. My friend asked if they had a bit more worktop, to which the man said yes, a small piece. My son then went on to build a bespoke kitchen; everything fitted perfectly. I had once again been reminded that you need to stick to the blueprint!

The little shop was now painted on the inside, it had a lovely kitchen, a beautiful oak counter and a wonderful laminated floor. It was amazing; now I needed a plumber to come and plumb in the new Butlers sink.

This was going to be around £300 to £400. I was discussing it with my friend, the trustee of the land, and she said she'd been watching me as this project had been going on and had noticed that whatever figure I believed God for, I seemed to get. She thought I should believe God for £500. She suggested a sale on the green, so I agreed with her that we would pray together and believe in God for £500 and have a sale. The next couple of weeks, we set about getting bits and pieces together. I went to a few garden centres and was given plants, my friend was gathering bric-a-brac and other friends from Women of Light baked cakes for the occasion.

The day of the sale, I looked at the tables laid out with all the goods to sell, and the teas and wonderful cakes. I remember looking at the pretty impressive spread and thought there's not £500-worth of goods here to sell. But I was really excited to see how the Lord was going to do it. It wasn't for me to work it out. I had prayed in faith with my very dear friend that God was going to do it.

We had a really good turnout; it was a lovely sunny day in July 2009. People kept turning up and donating cakes and more things to put on the stalls. There was a real buzz, with the sound of chatting, mixed with laughter. Children were playing, people were turning up with their dogs. It was a really busy afternoon. We sold lots of cream teas, and cake. Everyone really enjoyed themselves and were looking forward to The Light House being completed and open for business.

After the last person had left, the friend who I had prayed with sat down to count the money. She laid it all out on the counter. We had also been given two small cheques as donations to The Light House. Finally, my friend had counted the money and it was £497. I laughed because I had somebody buy cream teas but when they came to pay, they had realised that they didn't have their purse with them and said they would give it to me in church on Sunday. The following week at church I was handed £2 for the teas, and I didn't have the heart to say it was £3! We now had £499.

Back at The Light House, I was just admiring the new steps down from the veranda which my son had made a few weeks before, when I saw something on the ground – it was gold, and shining. I bent down to pick it up. It was a £1 coin. I laughed. We now had the £500 for which we had been believing. What an amazing God we have! My friend and I rejoiced; he had done it! He had done it again. Our faith was greatly increased.

Not long after this I was working at The Light House when I had a visit from the vicar. He had come to tell me that he was leaving the parish. He had been given an opportunity to serve in another area, which was several hours away. I was sad but if I had known his position as vicar was a temporary one, I probably would have stayed where I was and therefore would never have had the vision for The Light House!

After the vicar left, I too decided that I would leave that church and finish The Light House meetings on a Friday. I would concentrate on what the Lord had called me to do at The Light House shop.

I then joined another traditional church with a few of the young mothers who had been on the Alpha course.

Chapter Eleven: The Shop

I continued with the vision and reminded myself of the purpose of The Light House. It was being a light in the village and putting the heart back into the community, a meeting place.

I knew it had been run as a shop before and had gone out of business, as it was not viable to just be a village shop; I realised why I had had a picture of teacups and saucers – it was to be a tearoom. I would need to work there full-time. I would need a wage to live and cover the cost of rent on my cottage, plus pay the utility bills on the shop. So, once I had worked out how the village stores and tearoom would be run, I had to share the vision with my friends and recruit volunteers from the village and Women of Light, and any of my friends who wanted to be involved. I now knew how it would be run as a shop and tearoom, and it needed to be fitted out for the purpose.

I shared the vision with friends and those at Women of Light who had been watching how the Lord had been providing for the renovation of the shop. One of the trustees of The Light House gave me a beautiful Welsh dresser. Another friend from Women of Light who had been a great support to me during the renovation period of the shop, bought a freezer with an ice cream dispenser with the local schoolchildren in mind. I went to IKEA and bought the wooden tables and chairs for the inside, and a friend bought the outside tables and chairs to go on the veranda. Then someone else donated a bench for the veranda and a table.

My friend who was the trustee of the land took me to a wholesaler and bought the china for the shop. On the way home we saw an old chiller cabinet outside a shop, and we decide to phone them and ask if we could have it. They said we could, but it was old, so my friend decided that we needed a new one, which she bought.

I also bought big baskets to put in fresh produce, cafetières for fresh coffee and glass domes to put over the cakes. Then my son came in and put up shelves. We were given a wood burner, but it was going to be too expensive to install, so we were then bought an electric heater in wood-burner style, with a chimney. I made a children's corner with a little wooden dresser with teacups on it and a children's table. We would also put toys out on the green for children.

As this work was going on, I had a lady from the village approach me. She was a Christian and wanted to be involved, and she also attended Women of Light. I had many of the Women of Light people coming forward offering to do shifts, and I had people offering to make scones and different things to eat. Also, some of the locals wanting to be involved and volunteer.

So, it was all really starting to come together very fast now. I then needed to contact suppliers. I was wanting fresh bread daily, and cakes. I found a local ice cream supplier and a local dairy for a milk delivery. We would stock the chiller cabinet with milk, butter and cheese. I then found a lady in the village to supply fresh eggs and a man to provide local honey. Then, to fill the dresser and shelves I would need stock, and I found a company that put our branding on the labels; everything would have The Light House on it. We had jars of jams, marmalade, chutney, cheese, biscuits in lovely tins, packs of shortbread, a selection of packets of biscuits, all with our branding, and jars of old-fashioned sweets. We would sell packs of coffee from the selection of coffees that we served from a local coffee supplier, and we would also sell a selection of teas from another supplier. I was now happy that I had sourced all that I needed.

I got a bookkeeper in place, and I printed out recording sheets, the same as I had used at the charity shop I had managed. A friend bought a till. I then went on a food hygiene course and was shown how to fill out the daily forms which were needed to record the temperature of the fridge and chiller cabinet, names of food suppliers and so on. We bought a soup kettle like a big cooking pot as I was going to make homemade soups daily.

I would meet friends at the shop to pray for the new adventure that was just about to begin. One day I prayed and asked the Lord what I was to do next, and he said, 'I want you to book a hall in the village and invite the whole village to come and hear why The Light House is there. I want you to invite a guest speaker to come and share a powerful testimony of how I have changed a life to bring them from darkness into light.' The same as we did at Women of Light. Before the speaker came to speak, I would share the vision of The Light House with the people, how we were going to put the heart back into the community, to provide a meeting place, and we would be providing a village stores and a tearoom. We were a Christian presence within the village. I asked the Lord who he wanted me to invite to come and share their story. A man came to mind, someone that I had not personally met but knew about through the friends. I only knew him as the 'jelly fish' man who had a very powerful testimony. He was from New Zealand and had been out surfing and was stung by box jellyfish. He had been officially pronounced dead and had been put on a mortuary slab but had a heavenly encounter with Jesus, and came back to life.[37] I was wondering how I would ever track this speaker down, and would he be available to come to our village hall? But I knew if he was the person the Lord had asked me to invite, I would find him.

Amazingly, only a few weeks later, I found out he was coming to speak at a village the other side of the Downs from where we were. The chances of that happening were slim, but of course, the Lord already knew he was coming; this was confirmation that Ian McCormack was our speaker. My friend and I drove to the village hall where he was speaking and we

37. See https://www.aglimpseofeternity.org/ (accessed 1 November 2022).

heard him share his powerful testimony. Once the meeting was over, I waited for my chance to speak to him. I went up and introduced myself and my friend, and I told him that the Lord had laid him on my heart. I was to invite him to come and speak, did he have any dates available? He was absolutely sure he was fully booked, but I politely asked him to check his diary! He looked at his schedule, and then confirmed that there was in fact one date that had a question mark over it. This was in two weeks' time. With that I said, 'That's my date! Can you put my name and phone number by it?' He later confirmed that it was our date and the others had cancelled! Now all I needed to do was book the hall.

I had learned another lesson you need to be persistent, like the persistent woman in the Bible in Luke 18:1-8; she didn't give up. I had also learned from Women of Light that when God tells you to invite a speaker, he has the date and hall lined up, and he already knows who's coming. The Lord gave me the blueprint for the evening – what food we were to prepare and even how the tables should be laid out. Instead of fresh flowers, the Lord told me to put out lanterns with lighthouses on them and light them, but where would I get such a thing? I only had ten days to organise the event. I asked the Lord where I would get them, and he told me a shop on the seafront sold them. I went and bought up all their stock.

I made flyers about the coming meeting at the village hall with a phone number on them to book seats. I let all my church contacts know about the up-and-coming evening meeting, with dinner, and it was open to men and women. The phone started ringing and we were soon fully booked. More than 100 people were coming!

The food was cooked and brought to the hall and kept hot until served. It was a wonderful evening. All the volunteers set about doing their separate tasks. The tables were all laid out beautifully, just as the Lord had shown me. Each table had a lighted lantern with a lighthouse on it, the name of the shop spiritually signifying our presence as a beacon of light. I remember when the speaker arrived, he was amazed at how well organised we were, having only had a short time to arrange everything. But of course, I have learned that all we need to do is stick to the blueprint and it's easy! It was an amazing evening, with some people coming to know the Lord for the first time, and it was a wonderful opportunity to share the vision.

Finally, the day of the opening came. We were all so excited! All the preparation was over and we were about to open the door to the community for the first time. I prayed about who should cut the ribbon to the new stores and the Lord showed me Milly. After all, it had been Milly's deep desire to keep the village stores open and for them not be demolished.

It was a beautiful sunny day. People turned out after having waited for so many months, watching the transformation taking place of the poor, little, neglected building! Now standing proud in beautiful parkland, it was a wonderful fulfilment of God's vision, this beacon of light. Milly was dressed in her pretty pale-blue suit, with scissors in hand, poised to cut the ribbon. As she cut it, up went a loud cheer. Then it was over to me to thank the many people for their continual support, in so many ways, and to God be the glory.

My youngest daughter joined me working in The Light House, as she had been with me on so much of the transformational journey and, with my group of volunteers, she was now just wanting to serve the local community.

So, The Light House began. We had lots of people coming from far and wide, so it was a very busy place, and became a favourite haunt for many to enjoy the beautiful surroundings, with the majestic presence of a horse chestnut tree that stood just outside with a bench winding round the trunk. In May and June, we would see it in full bloom, the flowers on the tree all standing tall, then in the hotter months, we would sit under its huge canopy for shade, with a pot of tea and homemade scones, strawberries and cream.

People would be seen sitting on the pretty veranda overlooking the park, with hanging baskets, and taking in the scent from the roses as they walked up to the entrance of the little timber building. There was one seat that people always wanted first and it was the bench round the side of the shop; it could seat two people, had big cushions on it and a low table just in front. Entering the building, it was a beautiful sight – the tables with freshly cut seasonal flowers, the shelves packed with all kinds of treats, both sweet and savoury; they would be bought as a treat to take home. We had beautiful cards that we sold, pictures of the little store, a memento of their visit. Up at the polished oak counter we had homemade cakes under glass domes and baskets of freshly baked scones. We always had wonderful music playing in the background. We used to get groups that had walked the South Downs and booked in advance with their orders, dog walkers and a lot of church groups. I always remember one minister, fascinated by how busy the shop was, asking how we got so many people. I said, 'Oh, the Lord brings them.' But most importantly, how did we serve the local community? We would have grandparents from the village coming regularly with grandchildren, who loved to sit and play at the table in the children's corner with the tea set, or playing outside with the toys, or on the swings in the children's park. We also had many young mothers. The WI group met at the shop once a week in the afternoon, had tea, and knitted and chatted over whatever they were doing.

We were a regular meeting place for parents after school for a cuppa and a chat, and the children would queue for their ice creams in all weather. It was a place that the locals could always come and meet friends and neighbours for a coffee in the morning, with the fresh cheese scones made by a Woman of Light lady; they were a favourite and were always sold out. We had the local policewoman, too, who had a surgery once a month, where local people could come and ask questions or report anything suspicious. We had people who lived alone coming in for a chat and making new friends. And often we had people who just needed a listening ear.

My neighbour next door to the shop made jam that I bought and used with the cream teas, which was our most popular tea. He in turn gave the money to a charity. I was selling so many fresh eggs that the woman in the village I bought them from had to increase her flock to keep up with demand. We also had a fresh bread delivery every day, milk and the basics for the villagers. We would have evening events, and carols outside at Christmas with hot chocolate and mince pies. And when the snow was thick on the ground, we would take out a sledge laden with goods and visit the locals, who were always pleased to see us and grateful that we had come.

I think we were seen as that beacon of light in the village, and it was a really great privilege to be the lighthouse keeper and serve in that place. One of my favourite pictures, if I had to choose one, would have to be Milly sitting across the table with a large scone cut into small pieces to share with her little friend, who was only two years old, the daughter of one of my volunteers. Much to Milly's delight, they were best of friends, Milly chatting away as the little girl tucked into her scone, her head barely reaching the tabletop. To me this had always been one of the most important aspects, how I had always seen The Light House, old and young alike, sharing friendship. Milly's prayer in that tiny prayer meeting all that time before had been answered in such an amazing way. Milly was always singing; she made everyone that knew her smile. I often knew she was coming before she arrived as I could hear her singing as she walked up to the shop. Most days she would come for a pot of tea, and sometimes she would say she had come to volunteer and roll up her sleeves to help with the washing up or take a tea towel and dry up the crockery from the lunchtime rush.

I had been given details of another lady, and had been asked to visit her. She had had a stroke and was living downstairs in her cottage. I would visit her once I had locked up, and sometimes I would bring her to the shop. But best of all she loved to come out with me in the car, while I did the banking and picked up cakes from the bakery. She would reminisce about her childhood and would tell me stories of her life in the village. We also helped the elderly who could no longer get to the shops by picking up groceries that they needed, and we didn't stock. I was also looking after two little girls who had started at the village school; both parents worked, so the girls would be dropped off early in the morning where we would play, or I would pull out the large craft box I had made up for them. They always had a snack, then I would then walk them up to the local village school, where many of the children knew me from their afternoon visits to the shop.

I remember the little stone church in the village; it was beautiful inside, it even housed William Morris tiles. One night the Women of Light team that came with me to pray in the villages arranged to have a meeting there, and one of their husbands came too, and gave his life to the Lord. So often in the past I would think, 'What happens to people that you lead to Christ?' and the Lord always said the same thing, 'If they really want to know me, I will reveal myself to them' – just as he is still doing in my life.

Chapter Twelve: New Beginnings

I was very busy with the Women of Light meetings, and The Light House. This was a very happy season in my life. I used to meet with friends and pray. I had a few single friends who wanted to find husbands and get married and they would often ask me to pray for them, which I would always do. At one of these prayer meetings, one friend asked me why I never prayed for a husband for myself. I had never really thought about praying for a husband because I was so happy and never ever thought I would want to marry again. I felt like the Lord was my husband;[38] it was him that I loved most, and in him I would confide. Why would I want to marry again? I had always loved my husband and it literally broke my heart when our marriage was over; it had taken many years for the Lord to heal me. How would I ever be able to trust again?

But one night when praying with my single friends I did ask the Lord for a husband. If I am really honest, my heart wasn't in it. I didn't think that I really wanted one. I had been single for a number of years, and it had taken time to rebuild my life. I was loving having my life in God, so full of adventures.

Not many months after this prayer, I was in The Light House and Milly's daughter came in. We were talking, when she asked me if I was single. I said I was, and she said that I wouldn't be on my own for long. Did she know something I didn't? I think if someone is single, everyone assumes that that person wants someone!

It was that very night that I returned home to my little cottage very tired after a long day and a visit with an elderly lady on the way home. I went into the tiny sitting room and sank down into the well-worn leather armchair. My daughter was out, so I was quite alone in the cottage. Then I saw a picture in my mind's eye. It was a shock! I saw myself dressed

---

38. Isaiah 54:5.

167

as a bride in a wedding dress; I had a veil swept back off my face. It was me! I was a bride; I could see by my face I was happy. I was standing in the doorway of a house, peering out. The next thing I saw was a long driveway leading up to the house. I saw all my children with their other halves. I saw what looked like young twins. Everyone was smiling, all really happy. It was obvious to me that it was my wedding day. I just laughed. I laughed because I couldn't believe it. I couldn't have imagined it because it was not what I wanted. But I knew it was a picture from God.

The next day I told my friend who was one of my trustees what I had seen concerning the wedding. She shrieked with excitement and pointed out that when I said that I had seen a picture, those things come to pass. She had witnessed the Lord's provision in bringing The Light House into being, and Women of Light, and she was in no doubt that this was from the Lord, and it would happen. She then said she would buy a hat for my wedding and we both laughed.

I just carried on with my really busy life, and forgot about it, but over the next few years the Lord was to show me the same picture again. I would just laugh.

My youngest daughter was now wanting to move out and live with her boyfriend. I was starting to think about moving as this would be the time. I felt the Lord was talking to me about living the other side of the Downs to be nearer The Light House. But I was concerned about being too far from my daughter; I felt I needed to be nearby. But I had also felt the Lord was prompting me to live the other side of the Downs. I was wrestling with what to do and thought, 'Once my daughter moves out, I will make a decision where to live.' I felt that the Lord had laid the little cathedral town on my heart, so I decided I would view a property there. So I booked up with an agent to see a property right in the centre of town. When I got there I realised parking would be a problem, and the property was so small, it would have been hard to have my family come to stay. Other than the Lord, they were the most important part of my life. I remember saying to the Lord, 'I can't live there. I need to be able to have my family to stay.'

The months passed, my daughter had moved out and I was still in the cottage. I carried on living in there, going over the Downs to The Light House early in the morning. Life was busy between The Light House, Women of Light and prayer meetings. Once in the early hours of the morning I received a phone call from my daughter asking me to go round to her place, which I did, and I landed up taking her to hospital, only to find she was suffering from a panic attack.

I knew that the tenancy was coming up on my cottage and I should not renew it, but I should look for somewhere else to live; I was still wrestling with God about it. I decided that I would move out and store my furniture and stay with a friend while I made up my mind. She lived even further away from The Light House so I would need to decide my next move quite soon. I just remember crying to God one night, 'I can't do this any more! I need to find a home.' I was feeling very insecure. My friend was lovely, very kind and supportive, but I needed my own home. So, the next day I went and viewed a converted chapel not far from where my daughter lived. I made a quick decision to put a deposit on it, so that it was secured; it would be big enough for my family to stay, that's really all I cared about. It would be free in a month. I felt more settled now, having made my mind up about my living arrangements.

I had a phone call from a friend at that time telling me that a missionary couple who lived not far from The Light House were home from being overseas and that the wife, who I vaguely knew, would like to come and volunteer at The Light House. So, she came and was a great help. I could call her up at short notice and she could get to The Light House very quickly. She spent a lot of time there, and we prayed together. She knew that I was wanting to live near my daughter, and I felt the Lord was calling me to live this side of the Downs. She then said that when they went back overseas I could live in her house and pay a small rent, and I would be near the shop.

I thanked her for the offer, but I still wasn't sure. I didn't tell her I had already paid a deposit on the chapel. She suggested it to me again a few days later. The last time she asked, I thought, 'It won't hurt to look.' As I drove into the village it felt right; her home was a large family house, and she showed me the single room that I would have. I asked if my family would be able to come and stay at Christmas, and other times, to which she agreed; also I would need to use the internet for the Women of Light meetings. In the garden was an annexe with a tenant. She was a single Christian lady with whom I went on to become friends. A week later, my missionary friends went back overseas, and I moved into the house, losing my deposit on the chapel. The house was comfortable, but as the weather was changing it was becoming cold and the storage heater in the bedroom had stopped working. So, in the really cold weather I would sleep downstairs by the wood burner.

It was really good being so close to The Light House. I could leave later for work in the mornings and my daughter would come in before her shift in the old people's home nearby, where she worked.

During this period, we were having regular power cuts and that's when I met my next-door neighbour. He was an older man who had lost his wife a few years before, a widower, and my friend in the annexe would call and ask him to come and have a look at the electrics. He would often go to his second home in France, and rather than put his cat into a cattery, would ask my friend to come in and feed the animal.

It was winter; my daughter and her boyfriend had split up and she was now living with me. She worked a lot of night shifts, so she would sleep in the day in the cold single bedroom that I slept in at night. Once she was up, she would come and help me in The Light House. I was so glad that I had moved to this side of the Downs, as she was now living with me near her job. It became so cold that my daughter and I both started sleeping downstairs, trying to keep the wood burner going; we were freezing.

One morning we woke to find that there was thick snow on the ground. It was magical, very beautiful; the whole of the garden was covered in a thick white woollen blanket. You couldn't make out what some of the objects were, they were just white, having been covered by the snow, and some things had just disappeared; all we could see was white brilliant white, like wool. It made me think of the scripture in Isaiah 1:18: "'Come now, let us reason together,' says the LORD. "Though your sins are like scarlet, they shall be as white as snow; though they are red as crimson, they shall be like wool." Those objects were like us before Christ in our fallen, broken state. Then we, like the objects, are covered in the snow – washed 'in the blood of the Lamb' and given brilliant white robes of righteousness (Revelation 7:14). That's how God sees us; our sins are gone and all he sees is the whiteness, like the snow. Even the branches on the fruit tree outside the window were bent over under the weight of the snow. There was no sound to be heard, it was as if this white blanket had muffled all sound. We ventured outside and into the little porch. We could see our breath in front of us as we spoke. Putting on our boots, we could feel the crisp white blanket being crushed beneath our feet, making a crunching sound in every step we took towards my little black sports car, now just a large white object. We looked at the car and at each other and began to laugh; then my daughter bent down and gathered snow in her hands, rolling it into a ball, and proceeded to throw it in my direction. I too grabbed a handful of snow. Now the silence was broken and there was laughter as we dodged the snowballs.

Two of my neighbours came out to see what all the commotion was, and we stopped our game and told them we were just clearing the way for our car to get out. They helped us and my daughter and I jumped into the car and very carefully made our way to the shop. Our bread delivery had not been able to get through, so we drove to the bakery and collected our bread. We sat in the shop by the little wood burner, warming ourselves, but there wasn't a soul in sight.

'What shall we do?' my daughter asked.

'Well,' I replied. 'If the village can't get to us, then we will go to the village!' We borrowed a sledge, piled it high with goods and went to every home in the village. Most people wanted something and were glad that we had come. At the end of the day, we gathered up some bread and milk and took it to some of our elderly neighbours. My friend in the annexe had been stranded and was unable to get into work; she was really pleased that we had brought her some fresh bread and milk too. And finally, I left some bits on our next-door neighbour's doorstep.

The snow went on for a few more days. One night, not long after the snow was beginning to thaw, I had returned home and my neighbour knocked on the door. He had helped me get the car out of the drive twice that week, and now was coming to thank me for the bread and milk. Then he asked if I would like to go to dinner at his house, and he would also invite my friend in the annexe and her new boyfriend. I agreed that I would come.

The next evening, I walked round to his house to find that my friend from the annexe and her boyfriend were already there in the sitting room by the large wood burner. It was a lovely evening, very light-hearted, and we laughed a lot. Our host had made the most delicious meal and we all appreciated the effort he had put in. The conversation got on to the subject of how my friend had met her boyfriend. They said they had met online, and I laughingly said, 'I could never do that!' It was a really amusing evening, and we all agreed that we should it again sometime.

From that evening on, my neighbour used to come round most days to see if he could chop wood for the wood burner, or even light the fire, check the car over, or ask me if I would like to come to dinner! I remember the first time that I went to dinner at his house on my own. He had spent the whole of the afternoon following a recipe and had made an amazingly tasty fish pie, which went on to become his signature dish.

My neighbour – a Christian man – and I went on to become really good friends we spent a lot of time together when we weren't working. We both had large families. He had three children and of course, I had four. He also had a young grandson who lived overseas. Then I received the news that my eldest daughter was now expecting a baby. This was really exciting. I could hardly wait to become a grandmother; it was 2009 and I was now forty-eight years old.

I was still busy at The Light House and with Women of Light. I was going into hospital in a month's time, so I was having to make lots of arrangements for who would be covering shifts, ordering stock weekly, writing up the daily sheets and so on. There was a lot to do, with the upcoming Women of Light breakfast to organise as well. I had the operation, and I was off work for five weeks. My neighbour would come round at least three times a day to check that I had everything I needed, and that is when we realised we were falling in love. Over the coming months we were not often apart, and he asked me to marry him, which I did a few years later.

We have seen four of our children married in the time we have been together. So now all seven children are married, and we have fourteen grandchildren, nine of which are mine. In my nine, I have a set of twins and my husband has five grandchildren.

On the day of our wedding, we had a photograph taken in a hurry, on the long driveway leading up to the house, with all of our children in the drive and two little girls dressed the same. They looked like twins but of course they weren't; one was my granddaughter, and one was my husband's. But I do have twins now, born to my daughter. Of course, when I look back at the photos after the wedding, the only picture taken at home was on our long driveway. This was just as I saw in my vision about my wedding! I laughed. I am so glad that God had his way to which side of the Downs I should live. It is amazing how God works out plans for our lives.

Now, I am living in a small village in North Yorkshire. My husband and I moved here when he retired, and two of my children and grandchildren are also here. The Light House was sold and has a new name, still a shop serving the village.

Where I now live is an area of outstanding natural beauty. As I write, it's the autumn and the distinctive chill is in the air again; I walk daily with the Lord while walking my two springer spaniels. They are always so full of zeal. They love life and always enjoy it, whatever the season.

We are in the rutting season, and we often see the mighty stag with his harem, in an opening deep within the bracken, which at the moment is bright orange, rust colour; the heather is fading, having filled the moors with its purple haze. The mountain ash trees still have bright red berries – God's larder for the winter's wildlife. The grouse, red-legged partridge, and the pheasants often grace us with their presence. Every morning I stand high up on the rocks and admire the view. I can see the village, the fields with their stone walls and the sheep sheltering from the wind. Or I walk in the woods, which at the moment is ablaze with colour, all in different phases of transition as they leave the hot summer behind. It's like walking through a cathedral with stained-glass windows where the sun is shining, like shards of light piercing through the trees.

I can hear the sound of the water, the little stream running alongside my path. I watch the ducks as they dive under the water and then bob up to the surface again, having held their breath for what seems like an age. The red deer peeping at us from their home in the forest stand still like statues then, all of a sudden, they make a dash, and I see them disappearing deep into the forest. My dogs, Pippin and Horace, can resist it no more and jump into the stream for their daily dip, then out again, shaking themselves, the water flying everywhere. I take cover and laugh, only for them to do it again. Then I walk the path and talk to the Lord, where I love to be most.

Having come through the COVID-19 pandemic I am happily settled into a church family, and I am poised and excited about my next adventure in God. There are many villages all around me and I long to see them filled with light. I will pray for the blueprint.

Author's Note

I hope as you have read this book, you have had a glimpse of my beautiful, wonderful, exciting God, who sent his Son to die on the cross for you, and for me, so that we might have a relationship with him.

If you feel you would like to have a relationship with him, then there is a little prayer just for you to say here, so that you too can start your journey into life.

You could start by asking the Lord to become your shepherd, and that's what he will do. You will know his voice. So don't worry about being misled; the Bible tells us in John 10:5: 'But they will never follow a stranger; in fact, they will run away from him because they do not recognise a stranger's voice.' In John 10:14, Jesus tells us, 'I am the good shepherd; I know my sheep and my sheep know me'. It is having that perfect relationship with the shepherd, with Jesus, who knows you. He knows everything about where you have come from and where you're going.

Even through your journey will have highs and lows, one thing I can tell you is that he will 'never ... leave you' (Hebrews 13:5); the shepherd is always there.

Psalm 23

The LORD is my shepherd, I shall not be in want.

He makes me lie down in green pastures,

he leads me beside quiet waters,

he restores my soul.

He guides me in paths of righteousness for his name's sake.

Even though I walk through the valley of the shadow of death,

I will fear no evil,

for you are with me;

your rod and your staff,

they comfort me.

You prepare a table before me in the presence of my enemies.

You anoint my head with oil;

my cup overflows.

Surely goodness and love will follow me all the days of my life,

and I will dwell in the house of the LORD for ever.</q>

Prayer:

Dear Lord Jesus, I ask you to forgive me for the things that I have done wrong in my past life.

[Stop and think for a minute. Maybe name a few things.]

I know I need a Saviour and I am asking you to please wash my sins away.

I invite you into my life. Please come and make your dwelling in me.

I want to know you as my shepherd.

Amen.